LEARN LATIN

LEARN LATIN

The Book of the **Daily Telegraph** *QED* Series

Peter Jones

Duckworth

Second impression March 1997
First published in March 1997 by
Gerald Duckworth & Co. Ltd.
The Old Piano Factory
48 Hoxton Square, London N1 6PB
Tel: 0171 729 5986
Fax: 0171 729 0015

A catalogue record for this book is available
from the British Library

ISBN 0 7156 2757 0

Typeset by Ray Davies
Printed and bound in Great Britain by
Redwood Books Ltd, Trowbridge

CONTENTS

CONTENTS

CONTENTS

PREFACE

The purpose of this little book is to provide its users with enough Latin to read some poems of Catullus (1st century BC) and the *Carmina Burana* (13th century AD), and prose selections from the Bayeux tapestry (11th century AD) and St Jerome's version of St John's Gospel (4th century AD).

It owes its genesis to the imagination of Charles Moore, who as editor of the *Sunday Telegraph* and then of the *Daily Telegraph* commissioned a weekly introduction to Latin and oversaw its serialisation as a column in the *Sunday* (September 17 – December 24 1995), and (in new, expanded format) in the *Daily* (October 19 1996 – March 1 1997).

This revised and expanded version of the *Daily Telegraph* series is a result of reader demand. To the thousands who have written to me about the column, my best and warmest thanks. I am delighted to say that Duckworth will be publishing an ancient Greek *QED* in the same style and format (early 1998).

The audio-cassette pronunciation tape tied to the course, *Pronouncing Latin*, is available only from L.M.H. Jones (Tape) at the Newcastle Department of Classics. Cheques for £5 made out to L.M.H. Jones (to include p. and p.).

Peter Jones
Department of Classics,
University of Newcastle on Tyne
NE1 7RU
January, 1997

INTRODUCTION

The Latin language

Western civilisation is built on three mighty foundations – Greek, Jewish and Roman. Each made its unique contribution to the world we inhabit today.

But it was the Romans that made it all possible. The Roman empire and its great universal language, Latin, provided the means by which Jewish (and so Christian), Greek and Roman ideas and culture could spread throughout the West.

As a result, Latin is one of the most influential languages in the world. It has had a powerful and lasting effect upon nearly all European languages, including our own basically Germanic language, English.

Latin was also the language of education, church and state in Europe for 1500 years. Its literature has been enthralling readers for 2000 years.

Further, Latin is a superb educational tool. It is universally recognised as one of the best ways of learning *about* language, as all who have ever learned it will know.

We are now paying a high price for Latin's demise. While countries like France, Denmark, Holland, Italy, Luxembourg, Hungary, Romania and Spain continue to enjoy its benefits, we have cut a vital link with one of Europe's formative languages, literatures and cultures.

The purpose of this little book is to introduce you to Latin. It will not teach you the whole of Latin. What it will do is teach you enough Latin for you to be able to read selections from four major works – some poems of the greatest Roman love poet Catullus, the Bayeux tapestry, some of the *Carmina Burana* (set to music by Carl Orff in 1937) and extracts from St Jerome's Bible (the Vulgate).

Each chapter also contains features on Roman history, life and culture, and the influence of Latin on English. We trace the growth and decline of Rome's power, examine the personalities that made her great, explore aspects of her culture, and consider the nature of the impact of Latin on the English language (and other linguistic issues).

Here, then, is an unmissable opportunity for young and old to get a taste of this remarkable world and its language – and what a language it is!

The Roman Empire at its peak stretched from Britain in the west to Syria in the east, from the Rhine in the north to Egypt in the south. In the west it lasted 600 years, in the east nearly 1700 years (till Ottoman Turks took Constantinople [Istanbul] in 1453). Everywhere the Romans went, they took their language with them, and in the west, Latin became widely entrenched as the *lingua franca*.

So today, six hundred million people round the world speak a Latin-based language. French, Spanish, Portuguese and Italian are all directly descended from Latin.

English is slightly different. It is the language of the Anglo-Saxons. They entered Britain from the Germanic-speaking Denmark/ Holland/north German area from the 4th century AD onwards, when the Romans had left. The Danish 'swamp-corpses', sacrificial victims discovered in peat bogs, were Angles, our ancestors.

So English is basically a form of German. The major injection of Latin into English came, via French, with the arrival of William the Conqueror, Duke of Normandy, in AD 1066.

That is why our language is uniquely rich and subtle, and its vocabulary so huge. We have both German-based and Latin-based words for almost everything, e.g. king (German *König*) but regal (Latin *rex*), father (German *Vater*) but paternal (Latin *pater*), and so on.

Consider the start of the Lord's Prayer in English, Latin and the Latin-derived (Roman-ce) languages:

Our Father, which art in Heaven.
Pater noster, qui es in caelis (Latin).
Padre nostro, che sei nei cieli (Italian).
Padre nuestro, que estás en los cielos (Spanish).

Pare nostre, que estau en lo cel (Catalan).
Pai nosso, que estás nos céus (Portuguese).
Notre père, qui es aux cieux (French).

Note English 'father' (Germanic), but Latin *pater* gives us 'paternal', 'padre'; English 'heaven' (Germanic), but Latin *caelum* gives us 'celestial'.

Pronunciation

How do you pronounce an ancient language?

Astonishingly, we do in fact know fairly accurately how someone like Julius Caesar (100-44 BC) would have pronounced individual words. The accompanying audio-cassette *Pronouncing Latin* gives some idea (see Preface for the purchase of this tape).

To start with, Caesar would have pronounced every syllable. Thus *amare*, 'to love', *amahray*.

He would have pronounced 'c' hard, like 'k'; so too 'g', as in 'got'; he would have pronounced 'v' like 'w'; 'ae' as in 'eye'; 'i' short as in 'hit' *or* long as in 'wee'; and 'qu' as 'kw'.

Thus *vaco* 'I am free' (cf. vacation) = 'wackoh'; *caelum* 'heaven' (cf. celestial) = 'k-eye-lum'; *vaccae* 'cows' (cf. vaccine) = 'wack-eye'; *viri* (cf. virile) ='wi-ree'; *Vergilius* (Virgil) = 'Wheregillius'; *quae* = 'kw-eye'.

One important source of evidence for this is the way other languages spelled Latin. Thus ancient Greeks, who had no 'c', wrote *Cicero* as *Kikeron*, not *Siseron*. So we can be certain that Latin 'c' was pronounced hard. In time, of course, 'c' softened (e.g. Latin *centum* became French *cent*), but our evidence suggests that this did not happen till *c.* 500 AD. The 'ch' pronunciation of 'c' by the way, and the Church pronunciation in general, is simply Italian, which Pope Pius X tried to impose on the whole Catholic Church in 1912.

Again, ancient Greeks wrote Latin *Valerius* as *Oualerios*. That suggests Latin 'v' was pronounced more like English 'w'. Metre too helps the argument. Latin *silva*, 'wood', is often scanned as three syllables ('sil-oow-a') – very difficult to imagine if 'v' was pronounced as in English.

11

So however much the words may sound to us like characters from the Seven Dwarfs, Julius Caesar did indeed say 'waynee, weedee, weekee' (*veni, vidi, vici*, 'I came, I saw, I conquered').

Over time, this too changed. Latin *vinum* 'weenum' became French *vin*, and a Latin grammarian of the 2nd century AD tells us 'v' was pronounced 'with friction' – good evidence that it was now sounding more like the English 'v'. W.S. Allen in his *Vox Latina* (Cambridge) tells the whole story.

As *Pronouncing Latin* explains, there are also issues of long and short vowels (e.g. *amas* was pronounced 'uh-mar-ss'). Long vowels (all others are short) are marked only in the *Recorded Vocabulary*, pp. 170-3.

Suggestions

Learning Latin will be fun, but hard work. It is much the best thing to learn it with a group of others, especially if one of the group knows some Latin already, however rusty it may be. Lay in stocks of *vinum* (Italian, of course) to stimulate the brain cells. Our word 'wine', of course, is the same word as Latin *vinum*. Wine-drinking, and so the word, was a habit picked up directly from the Romans.

There is a full grammar and vocabulary at the back of this book, but keeping notebooks yourself is very helpful, especially to record and help you learn new vocabulary (alphabetical, Latin-English and English-Latin) and grammar.

'RECORD' indicates that these words will be used again and should be recorded and learnt; 'note' means that these words appear in the passage for translation, but need not be recorded.

The answers are given at the end of each chapter. You may peep.

Note

There are many ways to skin a cat and many ways to write a simple, introductory Latin course. This one is constrained by the fact that it had its origins as a teach-yourself newspaper column, with restricted space and limited target. Users should note:

(i) I explain only what is needed to read the target texts. So, for example, you will not meet the future or future perfect tenses. I guess that anyone who completes the course will have covered about two-thirds of a GCSE course in Latin.

(ii) I have adopted a light-hearted, fairly traditional approach to learning Latin, with plenty of potty sentences to keep the spirit high. For the purpose of this course, I have taken the language to be universal, tied to no particular time or place – which in this course indeed it is not, covering Latin from the 1st century BC to the 13th century AD.

(iii) I apologise if younger users are shocked to find that they have to learn things like vocabulary and grammar. Latin is not a subject for sissies.

(iv) Those who wish to go the whole hog are recommended to buy P.V. Jones and K.C. Sidwell, *Reading Latin* (*Text* and *Grammar*), Cambridge 1985. This is an adult reading course that covers the whole language in full detail. The same authors' *The World of Rome* (Cambridge 1997) is an adult introduction to Roman history, life and culture.

Excellent books on Latin and English include: for adults, D.M. Ayers, *English Words from Latin and Greek Elements* (Arizona 1965); for fun, and young teenagers, A.J. Spooner, *Lingo* (Bristol Classical Press, 1988). There are many etymological dictionaries, e.g. E. Partridge, *Origins* (Routledge, 1966).

CHAPTER 1

A Touch of the Verbals

You begin by learning one-sixth of all you need to know about the Latin verb.

Good, regular language, Latin.

Definitions

1a A *verb* expresses an action (e.g. kiss, dress, run) or state (e.g. be, wait).

When you list the parts of the verb (I run, you run, he/she/it runs, we run, you run, they run), you *conjugate* it.

'I run' is called first person singular (1*s*), 'you run' second person singular (2*s*), 'he/she/it runs' third person singular (3*s*); 'we run' is called first person plural (1*pl*), 'you run' second person plural (2*pl*), 'they run' third person plural (3*pl*).

The *tense* of a verb is the time it refers to: I run (*present tense*), I shall run (*future tense*), and so on.

Verbs: conjugal rites

1b All Latin courses start with the present tense of *amo*, 'I love' (cf. Amanda, amorous, amateur etc). This is no exception. This type of verb is called *first conjugation*:

1*s*	*am-o*	'I love, I do love, I am loving'
2*s*	*am-a-s*	'you love, you do love, you are loving' (*singular*)
3*s*	*am-a-t*	'he/she/it loves, does love (etc.)'
1*pl*	*am-a-mus*	'we love (etc.)'
2*pl*	*am-a-tis*	'you love (etc.)' (*plural*)

15

3*pl*   *am-a-nt*   'they love (etc.)'
Infinitive *am-a-re* 'to love'

RECORD this in your notebook as follows: *am-o* 1v [i.e. 1(st) conjugation) v(erb)] *ama-re*, love. All first conjugation verbs end in *-o* with infinitive in *-a-re*.

Record the Latin verb on one line, and the meaning on the line below. There will be more of the Latin verb to insert later on.

1c The stem *am-* means 'love'.

The next letter *-a-* is the key vowel (interestingly, *am-o* was once *am-a-o*!).

The various *endings* indicate who is doing the loving (*-o* = 'I', *-s* = 'you' (*s*), *-t* = 'he/she/it', *-mus* = 'we', *-tis* = 'you' (*pl*), *-nt* = 'they').

Note: (i) Latin does not need to use 'I', 'you', etc, whereas English does.

(ii) each person has three possible meanings e.g. *amo* 'I love, I do love, I am loving'.

(iii) the infinitive, *amare*, is a fixed form: it never changes.

By the way, why 'conjugation'? Latin *coniugo* 1v, to yoke (*iug-*) together (*con-*) the various parts of the verb. The phenomenon of changing the endings of a word to express meaning is called 'inflection'. Latin is a highly inflected language. Not just verbs, but nouns and adjectives all change endings quicker than a politician her mind.

Note that in the (Latin) end is your beginning. We say 'I love' – Latin says 'love' (*am-*) 'I' (*-o*).

So 'watch your ending' is the best piece of advice to give the Latin beginner. Useful rule in life, too.

Exercise

Remember: watch your ending.

1. Translate each word three ways: *amamus, amant, amatis, amo, amas*.

2. Translate *amat* nine ways.

3. Translate with one word into Latin: we do love, they are loving, you (*s*) love, you (*pl*) do love, to love.

4. Now add *non*, 'not', and translate: *non amamus* ('not we-love', i.e. 'we do not love'), *non amant, non amat, non amatis*.

5. Likewise: they do not love (= 'not they-love'), she does not love, you (*pl*) do not love.

Vocabulary

1d These verbs are all first conjugation like *am-o*.

RECORD them as indicated at **1b**:

d-o 'I give', *equit-o* 'I ride', *festin-o* 'I hurry', *interrog-o* 'I question', *ministr-o* 'I serve', *nunti-o* 'I tell, announce', *port-o* 'I carry', *pugn-o* 'I fight'.

RECORD *et* 'and', *nunc* 'now', *semper* 'always', *sed* 'but', *hic* 'here'. These are all fixed forms.

Exercise

1. Translate into English: *sed semper pugnant, hic equitamus, nunc non portat, festinare, datis et nuntiatis, semper festinas, nunc interrogamus, portant et minstrant, dare, equitare amant.*

2. Translate into Latin: they always question, to tell, you (*s*) carry, now we do not give, she rides and hurries, you (*pl*) always fight, but he does not now serve, here they always announce, you (*s*) love to fight.

3. Who or what is an ignoramus (*ignoro* 1v)? And what is its plural?

Answers

Please note: Latin-into-English answers are flexible. Only one answer is given, but others are possible, e.g. *amat* could mean he/she/it: loves/does love/is loving.

1c 1. We love; they love; you (*pl*) love; I love; you (*s*) love.

2. He/she/it//loves/does love/is loving.

3. *amamus, amant, amas, amatis, amare.*

4. They do not love, he does not love, you (*pl*) do not love.

5. *non amant, non amat, non amatis.*

1d 1. But they always fight, here we ride, now he does not carry, to hurry, you (*pl*) give and announce, you (*s*) always hurry, now we question, they carry and serve, to give, they love to ride.

2. *semper interrogant, nuntiare, portas, nunc non damus, equitat et festinat, semper pugnatis, sed nunc non ministrat, hic semper nuntiant, pugnare amas.*

3. It means 'we do not know'. Plural? Er ...

The world of Rome

From Romulus to the Empire

Most states boast heroic origins. Rome's were very nasty. It was founded and named by Romulus. Son of the hated war god Mars, he was cast out as a baby, suckled by a wolf, raised by shepherds, and later murdered his twin Remus when they quarrelled over the founding of the city. Romulus peopled Rome first by filling it with homeless vagabonds, then by seizing the womenfolk of the nearby Sabines ('the rape of the Sabine women').

Hardly a glorious beginning. But it is the way later Romans thought of their founding fathers – martial, dangerous, ruthless, practical. Whenever Rome was actually 'founded' – it was certainly inhabited by 1000 BC – by 295 BC it had brought all the tribes of the Italian peninsula under its control.

Rome was first drawn into extending its domains beyond Italy during the two 'Punic Wars' against Carthage (roughly Tunis – 264-202 BC). In the second of these, Hannibal came within an ace of bringing Rome to its knees. In 241 BC Rome created its first province in Sicily. North Africa, Spain, Greece and Asia Minor (Turkey) followed in the 2nd century BC; in the 1st century BC Gaul (France) – Julius Caesar's famous campaigns – Egypt and much of the near east (e.g. Syria); and in the 1st century AD, Britain. This is how the Latin language spread, the source of e.g. modern Spanish and French.

The genius of Rome was its ability to control such a vast empire with hardly any Roman manpower. They did this by 'romanising' the cities and cultures of each province's élites. The élites, not being able to beat 'em, joined 'em. They saw the economic and social advantages of being part of such a huge, powerful and successful enterprise. Romans were free with citizenship too, and liberal about local customs. As long as provincials paid their taxes and toed the line on Roman foreign policy, they were largely left alone.

Romans also knew a good thing when they saw it. For exam-

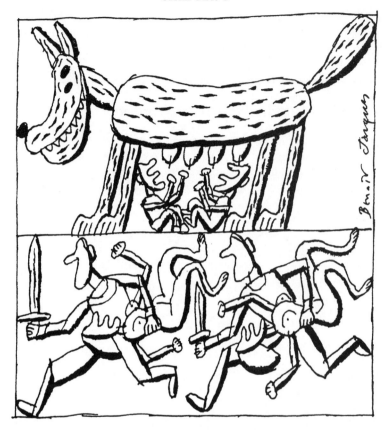

ple, they were bowled over by the Greek culture they met in the 2nd century BC, embraced it, made it their own – and ensured it was transmitted to us today. As the poet Horace famously said, 'Captive Greece took Rome captive, and brought culture to the Latin yokels'. This, for example, is why Roman ruins round the Mediterranean today always look so 'Greek': that was where Romans learned their architecture.

Word play

Britain was populated by Celts when the Romans made it a province of Rome in AD 43. When the Romans moved out in AD

410 and Anglo-Saxons from Denmark/Holland/north Germany moved in, the Celts drifted west, to Wales and Cornwall. They had picked up some Latin during the Roman occupation, as we can tell from modern Welsh and Cornish, e.g. Latin *pons* 'bridge', Welsh pont; *castra* 'camp' Welsh car or caer; *schola* 'school', Welsh ysgol.

The Romans had never conquered northern Europe, but the incoming Anglo-Saxons, who spoke a form of German, had still picked up some Latin through trade and other contacts. They brought with them to Britain words like street (Latin *strata*), butter (*butyrum*), mile (*mille*), wine (*vinum*), pin (*penna*), pillow (*pulvinus*), wall (*vallum*), sack (*saccus*) – the first Latin words in English.

CHAPTER 2

We indulge in more of the verbals

Already I hear murmurings from some of the young: 'one chapter gone, and I still cannot tell you my age in Latin, where I live and what pets I own. *And* I'm expected to *learn* things?'

Alas, all too true. These Romans were *hard*.

More conjugating

2a In the last chapter we looked at first conjugation verbs like *amo* 1v love. We saw the stem *am-* was followed by the key vowel *-a-* and the person endings *-o, -s, it, -mus, -tis -nt*.

You will now be thrilled to learn that there are four other conjugations. If at this point you decide you would rather do something simpler like quantum theory, let me remind you that Latin is a good, regular language.

The point is that the principle observed in the construction of *amo* (stem + key vowel + person endings) applies across the board to all the remaining conjugations. The only thing that changes is the key vowel. All you will need to remember is (wait for it) two new vowels: *-e-* and *-i-*.

So cancel that quantum theory course. The person endings (the things that *really* count for translation purposes) remain identical. *-o* continues to indicate 'I', *-s* 'you', *-t* 'he/she/it' etc. Difficult, or what? (See *Grammatical Summary* 6, 11, 16, 21 for the full listing.)

Second conjugation

2b Example: *mone-o* 2v I warn, advise.

Stem *mon-*, key vowel *-e-*, and off you go: *mon-e-o* I warn, *mon-e-s*, you warn *mon-e-t*, he/she/it warns (etc.), *mon-e-mus, mon-e-tis, mon-e-nt*. Infin. *mon-e-re*, to warn.

The signature of 2nd conj. verbs is *mone-o* + (infin.) *mone-re*.

Vocabulary

2c RECORD the following 2nd conj. verbs: *habeo* I have, *iubeo* I order, *teneo* I hold, take, *video* I see. Record as e.g. *habe-o* 2v *habe-re* I have.

RECORD also the fixed forms: *cur* why?, *quid* what?, *quis* who?

Exercise

Translate into English: *non habes, semper monent, quid iubetis?, tenes, videre, monemus, nunc habet, cur equitare amatis?, quis portat?, semper iubes, nunc non habent.*

Translate into Latin: you (*s*) warn, she sees, they love to take, we now have, they always hurry, who orders?, what do they advise?, you (*pl*) now question, to order, why does he take?

Third conjugation

2d Example: *reg-o* 3v I rule.

Stem *reg-*, key vowel *-i*: *reg-o, reg-i-s, reg-i-t, reg-i-mus, reg-i-tis, reg-unt*. Infin. *reg-ere* to rule. The only new thing here is the 3*pl* in *-u-nt*.

The signature of 3rd conj. verbs is *reg-o* + (infin.) *reg-ere*. Contrast 2nd conj. verbs *mone-o, mon-ere* at **2c**.

Vocabulary

2e RECORD *apprehendo* I seize, *dico* I say, speak, *duco* I lead, *mitto* I send, *traho* I drag, *vinco* I conquer. Record as e.g. *dic-o* 3v *dic-ere* I say.

Exercise

Translate: *quid dicis?, cur mittunt?, semper trahit, ducere amamus, nunc vincimus et apprehendimus, quis dicit?, mittimus, ducunt, trahitis, non ducit sed mittit.*

They always conquer, now we speak, what does he say?, we lead, they love to say, he seizes, you (*pl*) send.

Fourth conjugation

2f Example *audi-o* 4v I hear, listen.

Stem *aud-*, key vowel *-i-*: *aud-i-o, aud-i-s, aud-i-t, aud-i-mus, aud-i-tis, aud-i-unt*. Infin: *aud-i-re* to hear. Note again the 3*pl* in *-i-unt*.

The signature of 4th conj. verbs is *audi-o* + (infin.) *audi-re*.

Vocabulary

2g **RECORD** *nescio* I do not know, *scio* I know, *sentio* I feel, *venio* I come. Record as e.g. *nesci-o* 4v *nesci-re* I do not know.

Exercise

Translate: *quid sentis? veniunt, nescimus, audire amo, sentire, nunc scit, quis venit?, cur nescitis?, nescio sed sentio, hic venimus, quis nescit?*

We come, you (*s*) know, we feel, now they do not know, he knows but he does not come, who is listening? to feel, now they listen but they do not always know, we love to know.

Fifth conjugation

2h Example *capi-o* 5v I capture.

Stem *cap-*, key vowel *-i-*: *cap-i-o, cap-i-s, cap-i-t, cap-i-mus, cap-i-tis, cap-i-unt*. Infin: *cap-ere*.

The signature of 5th conj. verbs is *cap-io* + (infin.) *cap-ere*. Contrast 4th conj. *audi-o audi-re* at **2f**.

Vocabulary

2i **RECORD** *facio* I make, do. Record as *fac-io* 5v *fac-ere* I make, do.

Exercise

Translate: *non facimus, semper capit, quid hic facitis?, capere amat, faciunt, nunc quid facis?, cur auditis?, ducimus, quis regit?, capiunt.*

I do, to do, I feel, to feel, I capture, to capture, I see, to see, I rule, to rule, I carry, to carry.

Mixed bag

2j Now we get nasty – sorry, rigorous.

Here is a mixed bag of all conjugations, first to fifth, to translate. If you know the meaning of the stem and are confident about person-endings, you will find the Latin-English quite easy. But the English-Latin is different: you must also know the conjugation of the verb, and therefore what its key vowel is, and any wrinkles.

Take 'he leads'. Lead? Hmm – *duco*. Right. He? Mmmm – *t*. Right. So – *ducot*. Wrong. You need the stem of *duco*. That is *duc-*. Therefore *duct*? Wrong – you need the stem + key vowel. Key vowel is determined by conjugation. *duco* is 3rd conjugation. Key vowel is therefore -*i*- . Ah – *ducit*. Right.

Check carefully on 3rd *pl* -*unt*/-*iunt* in 3rd, 4th and 5th conjs.

Translate: *faciunt, audimus, mones, venit, vincunt, amatis, regis, scimus, dant, mittit, apprehendimus, habes, equito, ducitis, nuntias*; they lead, he seizes, we say, you (*s*) capture, she comes, we give, we have, they hear, they rule, they capture, you (*pl*) send, they say. Consult the *Grammatical Summary* sections 1, 6, 11, 16, 21 if you get into trouble.

Answers

2c You do not have, they always advise, what do you order?, you hold, to see, we warn, now he has, why do you love to ride?, who carries?, you always order, now they do not have; *mones, videt, tenere amant, nunc habemus, semper festinant, quis iubet?, quid monent?, nunc interrogatis, iubere, cur tenet?*

2e What do you say?, why do they send?, he always drags, we love to lead, now we conquer and seize, who speaks?, we send, they lead, you drag, he does not lead but sends; *semper vincunt, nunc dicimus, quid dicit?, ducimus, dicere amant, apprehendit, mittitis.*

2g What do you feel?, they come, we do not know, I love to hear, to feel, now he knows, who is coming?, why do you not know?, I do not know but I feel, here we come, who does not know?; *venimus, scis, sentimus, nunc nesciunt, scit sed non venit, quis audit?, sentire, nunc audiunt sed non semper sciunt, scire amamus.*

2i We do not make, he always captures, what are you doing here?, he loves to capture, they make, now what are you doing?, why do you listen?, we lead, who rules?, they capture; *facio, facere, sentio, sentire, capio, capere, video, videre, rego, regere, porto, portare.*

2j They do, we hear, you warn, he comes, they conquer, you love, you rule, we know, they gave, he sends, we seize, you have, I ride, you lead, you announce; *ducunt, apprehendit, dicimus, capis, venit, damus, habemus, audiunt, regunt, capiunt, mittitis, dicunt.*

The world of Rome

From rape to republic

In its early days, Rome was ruled by kings from the powerful neighbouring state of Etruria. But in 509 BC, Sextus, son of the king Tarquinius, took advantage of the trust reposed in him to rape Lucretia, a married Roman aristocrat. She committed suicide. The Romans rose in revolt and threw off their Etruscan overlords (celebrated in Macaulay's 'Lays of Ancient Rome' about how Horatius kept the bridge).

From then till 31 BC, Rome was a republic, ruled by officials

called 'magistrates'. They were elected for one year only by the whole Roman citizen body voting in 'colleges' – the top magistrates were the two consuls – and advised by the Senate (Latin *senex*, old man), consisting of all past magistrates. All laws they passed had to be brought back to the people again for their approval.

The Romans were hugely proud of this system of government (it was never a formal constitution, though the American constitution owes much to it). But in the 1st century BC it began to crumble, as men like Pompey and Julius Caesar chose to ignore this traditional way of doing things and use military might to impose their will on Rome. Romans were appalled. The crunch had come.

Word play

The main Latin influence on English between the arrival of the Anglo-Saxons and the 11th century AD was the Church. England became a Christian (catholic) country, and the influence of Church Latin and St Jerome's Latin version of the Bible (the 'Vulgate' – see **20b**) was enormous. At this time words entered the English language like minster (Latin *monasterium*), monk (*monachus*), nun (*nonna*), relic (*reliquiae*), cat (*cattus*), fork (*furca*), punt (*ponto*), trout (*tructa*), creed (*credo*), mass (*missa*), cook (*coquus*), camel (*camelus*), psalm (*psalmus*), lily (*lilium*).

The real turning point for English, however, was the conquest of the country by William, Duke of Normandy, in 1066 AD. The Normans (Norsemen, Northmen), an aggressive, restless and adventurous Viking people, had settled in northern France from the 9th century AD and within a hundred years had adopted its language, religion and customs. They were always on the lookout to expand, however, and Britain became the next target. After the Battle of Hastings (**19a**), the Norman French were to rule England for some 300 years.

CHAPTER 3

Bring on the nouns

We continue to beaver keenly away in the grammatical basement, but be assured we are digging secure foundations, on which real Latin literature will soon arise, shimmering in splendour. Next chapter, for example, we shall start constructing the damp-course for St Jerome's Latin Bible and the Bayeux tapestry (or embroidery, as it should really be called).

Nouns

3a 'Noun' derives from Latin *nomen*, name. Nouns give names to objects, ideas and people – chair, table; virtue, speed; Philippa, Phoebe and Tom. 'Pronouns' stand *for* (Latin *pro*) nouns – not Philippa or Phoebe but 'she', 'her', 'they', not Tom but 'he', 'him'.

3b Inspect the following very closely:
    1. *Corinna Deliam amat*: Corinna loves Delia.
    2. *Corinnam Delia amat*: Delia loves Corinna.
    3. *Delia et Corinna Lesbiam amant*: Delia and Corinna love Lesbia.
    4. *Corinnam amatis*: You (*pl*) love Corinna.
    Your conclusion?
    (a) When Corinna or Delia are *doing* the action, i.e. are subjects of the sentence, they take the form *Corinna/Delia* (called the 'nominative case' in Latin).
    (b) When they are on the *receiving end* of the action, i.e. are the objects of the sentence, they take the form *Corinnam/Deliam* (called the 'accusative case' in Latin).

29

(c) When two (or more) people make up the subject (sentence 3), the verb is plural (*amant* i.e. [they] love).

(d) The nom. case names the subject of the sentence. If there is no nom. case, as in 4 above, the subject is 'in the verb' – 'you', in this case.

3c You now know the most important thing there is to know about Latin nouns. In English, word *order* determines the meaning of a sentence: 'Corinna loves Delia' means Corinna is doing the loving (subject), Delia is on the receiving end (object).

But in Latin, word *form* determines the meaning of a sentence. When you see *Corinna*, you know she is subject of the sentence, wherever she appears in it. When you see *Corinnam*, she is object, wherever she appears in it. Thus *Deliam amat Corinna* can mean only one thing: Corinna loves Delia – because *Corinna* is in the subject-form, *Deliam* in the object-form. Put those same Latin words in any order, and they will still mean only one thing. But change *Corinna* to *Corinnam* and *Deliam* to *Delia*, and put them into any order, and the sentence will always mean 'Delia loves Corinna'.

Latin nouns, in other words, like Latin verbs, are 'inflected' (see **1c**): they change their endings to indicate the grammatical job they are doing. Watch your endings.

Exercise

Before you attempt this exercise, bear in mind three vital things.

(i) Latin word-order is not the same as English. In Latin, subject-object-verb ('Corinna Delia sees') is a very common order, but the words can in fact come in any order ('Sees Corinna Delia' etc.).

(ii) in English, the subject must come first ('Corinna'), then the verb ('sees'), then the object ('Delia').

(iii) if there is no noun in the nom. case, the subject is 'in the verb'. So go straight to the verb and begin there.

Note: Corinna, Delia and Lesbia are the names of the mistresses of the poets Ovid, Tibullus and Catullus respectively (if not respectably). Cleopatra is the last in the line of Ptolemies of

Egypt, the Greek kings and queens named after the first Greek ruler of Egypt, Ptolemy I (367-283 BC).

Cleopatra was pure Greek. She was the lover of Julius Caesar and Marc Antony. She and Antony committed suicide in 30 BC, after Octavian, Caesar's adopted son (later the first emperor Augustus), had defeated them in battle. From then on, Egypt was a Roman province.

Translate: *Lesbia Deliam amat; Delia Lesbiam non amat; Corinnam amamus* [note: the subject here is in the verb]; *O Lesbia, cur Cleopatram amas?; cur Delia Corinnam non amat?; Delia et Cleopatra Lesbiam amant; Corinnam amo; Deliam amatis; Corinna et Delia semper pugnant; Cleopatra Deliam interrogat; Corinna Deliam semper monet; Delia et Lesbia Cleopatram vident; cur Deliam mittis? quis Deliam venire iubet?* We lead Delia; but Lesbia questions Cleopatra; Gazza loves Corinna; Corinna always rules Delia.

Now translate these very carefully indeed, since they do not follow the normal Latin word order: *Cleopatram videt Delia; Corinnam non apprehendunt Delia et Lesbia; ducit Corinnam Delia; Lesbiam vincis et Deliam; Cleopatram amas capere.*

3d Nouns like *Corinn-a* and *Deli-a* end in -*a* in the nominative case and are called first declension (1st decl.). To decline Corinna (a dangerous thing to do) is to state Corinna's various (cough) forms, thus:

nom.: *Corinn-a* (subject of sentence)
acc.: *Corinn-am* (object of sentence)

Unless they are obviously male, all 1st decl. nouns are feminine (f.) in gender.

RECORD the following 1st decl. nouns, all declining like Corinna, in the form *Corinn-a n*.(oun) *1*(st) *f*(eminine) Corinna: *fortun-a n. 1f* luck, fortune; *aqu-a n. 1f* water; *eam* her (acc. f. only); *lun-a n. 1f* moon; *puell-a n. 1f* girl; *serv-a n. 1f* (female) slave; *stell-a n. 1f* star; *tenebr-a n. 1f* shadow; *terr-a n. 1f* land, earth; *vit-a n. 1f* life.

Note how every word (bar *puella*) gives us an English word.

Why, incidentally, 'decline/declension' and 'case?' Roman grammarians thought of the cases visually, with the nom. at the top and the others falling away ('declining') from it. 'Case' derives from the Latin *casus*, 'fall'.

Exercise

Important note: Latin has no word for 'the'. Sprinkle it around your translation as necessary.

Translate: *hic puella lunam et stellam videt; serva aquam dat; hic eam semper mittunt; Lesbia puellam et Corinnam ducere amat; cur vincis terram, o Cleopatra?; puella vitam amat; serva ad* ('towards', + acc.) *aquam venit; puella eam ad terram ducit; Cleopatra eam festinare iubet.*

Carmina Burana: O fortuna, velut (like) *luna, semper crescis* (*cresco* 3 – 'wax') *et decrescis* (guess!).

Answers

3c Lesbia loves Delia; Delia does not love Lesbia; we love Corinna; O Lesbia, why do you love Cleopatra?; why does Delia not love Corinna?; Delia and Cleopatra love Lesbia; I love Corinna; you (*pl*) love Delia; Corinna and Delia always fight; Cleopatra questions Delia; Corinna always advises Delia; Delia and Lesbia see Cleopatra; why do you (*s*) send Delia? who orders Delia to come?

Deliam ducimus; sed Lesbia Cleopatram interrogat; Gazza Corinnam amat; Corinna Deliam semper regit.

Delia sees Cleopatra; Delia and Lesbia do not seize Corinna; Delia leads Corinna; you (*s*) conquer Lesbia and Delia; you (*s*) love to capture Cleopatra.

3d Here the girl sees the moon and star; the slave gives water; here they always send her; Lesbia loves to lead the girl and Corinna; why do you conquer the earth, Cleopatra?; the girl loves life; the slave comes towards the water; the girl leads her to the land; Cleopatra orders her to hurry.

O fortune, like the moon, you always wax and wane.

The world of Rome

The first Roman emperor

Last chapter we saw how in the 1st century BC the much-vaunted Roman republican system – government by Senate and elected magistrates – was threatened by dynasts like Caesar and Pompey who, with armies at their back, ignored the constitution and struggled for power by military might.

In 49 BC Pompey banned Caesar from entering Italy with his

army. Caesar, saying 'the die is cast' – he knew he was taking a gamble – , crossed the river Rubicon (the technical boundary) and defeated Pompey in the ensuing civil war. Declaring himself effective dictator (some thought he was aiming to restore the hated kingship), Caesar was mown down by republicans on the Ides of March 44 BC – the signal for further civil war. In 31 BC Octavian, Caesar's adopted son and heir, emerged victorious.

Rome waited. Would the ghastly pattern of the last twenty years repeat itself? Octavian, renaming himself Augustus, saw to it that it would not. Claiming to reinstate full Senatorial authority and the annual cycle of magistrates, he drew all power into his own hands. Tactful, authoritative, wealthy, ruthless and a great propagandist, he persuaded the people and powerful Roman families that the republic had been restored. In fact, he became the first Roman emperor. He restored peace, Rome flourished again, and grateful poets like Virgil and Horace sang their new emperor's praises.

Word play

After the Battle of Hastings in 1066 AD and the Norman French occupation (which lasted till the 14th century AD), the English language underwent a radical transformation.

French is a Latin-based language. Julius Caesar had conquered Gallia (Gaul) in the 50s BC and made it a province of Rome, and the resident Gauls, unlike their British counterparts, had taken up the Latin language almost completely. Over the centuries it underwent various transformations, becoming less and less like Latin and more and more like what we know as French. After the Norman conquest, then, Latin-based French became the language of the English Court, government, schools and nobility, with dramatic consequences for English. This is essentially why English has such a rich and massive vocabulary – we have Germanic and Latinate words for almost everything, e.g. (Anglo-Saxon words first, Latin-based words second) motherly, maternal; drink, imbibe; high, elevated; sad, miserable; watch, observe; hate, detest; do again, repeat; hide, conceal; inner, interior.

Typical of the Latin-based words to enter English at this period are crown (*corona*), regal (*rex*), sermon (*sermo*), religion (*religio*), justice (*iustitita*), defendant (*defendo*), army (*arma*), navy (*navis*), study (*studium*), science (*scientia*), master (*magister*), doctor (*doctor*), cure (*cura*). These words were needed in the developing political, legal and educational world of the Middle Ages.

CHAPTER 4

We get St Jerome and the Bayeux
tapestry in our sights

More foundation digging this chapter, but you can look back and
say to yourself, 'Three solidly grammatical chapters and lo, we
are skirting the hem of the Bayeux tapestry and St Jerome's
Latin Bible already'. That is what these days we have to call
'adding value'. Can't think what's wrong with calling it 'making
progress', myself.

2nd decl. nouns in *-us*

4a Inspect the following. Only don't. You know how regular
Latin is. You met the principle of case-endings in the last
chapter, and will deduce the new nom. and acc. endings of the
new second declension (2nd decl.) nouns ending in *-us* with
laughable ease.

　　1. *Willelmus Haroldum vincit*: William conquers Harold.
　　2. *Willelmum Haroldus vincit*: Harold conquers William.
Yawn: tricky, or what?

4b　Here then are the 2nd decl. endings:
　　　nom.:　　*Harold-us* (subject)
　　　acc.:　　*Harold-um* (object)
Note that such nouns have a stem (*Harold-*) and endings (*-us* or
-um), just like 1st decl. nouns. They also remain true to type:
2nd decl. nouns have 2nd decl. endings.
　　RECORD the following 2nd decl. nouns: *angel-us* n. 2m angel;
Angl-us n. 2m Englishman; *De-us* n. 2m God; *Christ-us* n. 2m
Christ; *eum* him (acc. m. only); *fili-us* n. 2m son; *loc-us* n. 2m

Willelmvs Haroldvm vincit

place; *mund-us* n. 2m world; *Normann-us* n. 2m Norman; *serv-us* n. 2m (male) slave.

Note: 2nd decl. nouns are masculine (m.) in gender.

Exercise

All together, now, 'Watch your endings'.

Translate: *Anglus Normannum non amat; hic Normannus Anglum vincit; hic pugnare amant Anglus et Normannus; Deus nunc mundum et terram creat; Deus filium in* (into) *mundum mittit; nunc Deum et Christum angelus laudare amat; Deus mundum regit; Christus iubet, terra et mundus audiunt; cur Normannus Anglum non capit?; terram facit Deus; Haroldus eum locum apprehendere iubet; Christus in* (into) *mundum venit, et mundus eum nescit.*

2nd decl. nouns in *-um*

4c Another type of 2nd decl. noun ends in *-um* in the nom. All these are neuter (n.) in gender. Thus *bell-um*, war:

nom.:   *bell-um*
acc.:   *bell-um*

RECORD the following 2nd decl. n. nouns: *cael-um* n. 2n sky, heaven; *principi-um* n. 2n beginning, principle; *palati-um* n. 2n palace; *prandi-um* n. 2n dinner; *proeli-um* n. 2n battle; *vin-um* n. 2n wine.

Haroldvs Willelmvm vincit

Problem

4d You will at once have spotted a problem. You come across a noun ending in -*um*. Is it:

(i) nom. of 2nd decl. neuter, like *bellum*, and so subject?

(ii) acc. of 2nd decl. neuter, like *bellum*, and so object?

(iii) acc. of 2nd decl. masculine, like (e.g.) *servum*, and so object (*servus* being the nom.)?

Deep waters, Watson.

First check the dictionary. If the noun is 2nd decl. m. like *servus*, it must be acc. But if it is neuter, like *bellum*, it could be either nom. or acc., and only the context will tell.

E.g. *vinum palatium mittit. Vinum* and *palatium* are both neuter, so both could be subject or object. 'The wine sends the palace'? Or 'The palace sends the wine'? Surely the latter.

But cf. *servum palatium mittit. Servum* comes from *servus* and can only be object. Therefore 'The palace sends the slave'.

Rule: see -*um*, think, um ... .

Be warned: this sort of ambiguity will appear again. Romans, of course, did not intentionally construct grammatically ambiguous sentences (only modern, usually French, literary theorists do that, in their endless search for truth – or rather, ambiguity). But the ambiguities can be there for the beginner getting used to the language.

Exercise

Translate: *vinum, non proelium, amamus; caelum videre amant; filius semper prandium hic ministrat; vinum dat filius; Willelmus filium ad* (to + acc.) *bellum equitare iubet; hic facimus prandium; Normannus Haroldum apprehendit et ducit eum ad* (to + acc.) *locum et hic eum tenet; cur festinatis et palatium videtis?; Haroldus proelium nuntiat.*

Conjugal being: *sum* 'I am'

4e The verb 'to be' is as irregular in English ('I *am*, you *are*, he *is*') as in Latin. Here is the present tense, 'I am', *sum*.

Comparisons with French (derived from Latin) are added:

1*s*	*su-m* (je <u>suis</u>)	'I am'
2*s*	*es* (originally *es-s*) (tu <u>es</u>)	'you are' ;
3*s*	*es-t* (il/elle <u>est</u>)	'he/she/it/there is'
1*pl*	*su-mus* (nous <u>sommes</u>)	'we are'
2*pl*	*es-tis* (vous <u>êtes</u>)	'you are'
3*pl*	*su-nt* (ils/elles <u>sont</u>)	'they/there are'
Infin.	*es-se* (<u>être</u>)	'to be'

Note that while the stem changes back and forth from *su-* to *es-*, the personal endings remain regular. Ah! But what about *su-m*? Be not dismayed: you will find that the *-m* ending is a very common first person ending.

Do not use *sum* to translate e.g. 'I am loving'. The verb there is 'love', not 'am', and the answer is *amo*. (Note: the 'am' in 'I am loving', like the 'do' in 'I do love', is known as an 'auxiliary verb': Latin *auxilium*, help.)

Exercises

Translate: *estis, sunt, sum, est, sumus, esse*; she is, we are, we are sending, I am, they are, to be, they are riding, you (*s*) are, you (*s*) are warning, she is, she is giving.

Answers

4b The Englishman does not love the Norman; here the Norman beats the Englishman; here the Englishman and Norman love to fight; God now creates the world and earth; now the angel loves to praise God and Christ; God rules the world; Christ orders, the earth and world listen; why does the Norman not capture the Englishman? God makes the earth; Harold orders him to seize the place; Christ comes into the world and the world knows him not.

4d We love wine, not battle; they love to see the sky; the son always prepares dinner here; the son gives wine; William orders his son to ride to war; here we make dinner; the Norman seizes Harold and leads him to the place and here holds him; why do you hurry and see the palace?; Harold anounces the battle.

4e You (pl) are, they are, I am, he is, we are, to be; *est, sumus, mittimus, sum, sunt, esse, equitant, es, mones, est, dat.*

The world of Rome

The Roman Empire

In the last chapter we saw how in 31 BC the Roman republic ended in a bloodbath, and Augustus became the first Roman emperor.

The emperors had a pretty mixed reception from Roman historians. Augustus was often seen as the first of a series of tyrants. His successor Tiberius was portrayed as grouchy, suspicious, lazy and corrupt, spending his last years on Capri bathing with naked boys, Caligula as an incestuous pervert and lunatic murdered by his own guard ('how I wish you Romans all had one neck!' he once cried), Claudius as an ineffectual, slobbering cipher at the mercy of his wives, Nero (after a good start) as matricide, arsonist and (worst of all) artist, and so on.

One cannot whitewash this record. But something was going right. The empire prospered commercially, and even when serious internal feuds broke out, the system survived. For example, in AD 69, after Nero committed suicide and Galba succeeded, three generals in rapid succession staged coups to gain power.

Vespasian (legate of Judaea, who had also helped conquer Britain in 43 BC) finally won out. But the imperial system continued.

If the 2nd century AD was the great period of peace and prosperity, the 3rd century AD saw the empire under increasing pressure. In AD 395 Theodosius split it into two – the western half ruled from Rome, the eastern 'Greek' half from Constantinople (Istanbul). In the 4th century AD the mainly German immigrants in the west (who came essentially not to conquer but for the good life, and were usually easily absorbed) began carving out parts of the empire for their own domains, and the empire in the west effectively collapsed. That in the east, however, the 'Byzantine' empire as it was known (after Byzantium, the original Greek name for Constantinople) lasted till it was overthrown by Ottoman Turks on May 29 1453.

Word play

From the 16th century AD onwards, English borrowed more and more words directly from Latin, rather than inheriting them through French. A large number of these words were taken over to serve the expanding world of education, since it was felt that English was not developed enough to meet the demands of the new learning. New ideas and concepts demanded new words. Ancient Greek words too were taken on board for this reason. The first official, full-time university post in ancient Greek was estabished in Oxford in 1492.

Latin words taken over directly into English include e.g. (16th century) alias, arbiter, area, circus, delirium, genius, ignoramus, medium, radius, species; (17th century) census, curriculum, complex, lens, pendulum, series, specimen; (18th century) bonus, insomnia, propaganda, ultimatum; (19th century) consensus, omnibus, referendum. The borrowings from Latin and Greek in the medical and natural sciences at this time are, of course, gigantic.

CHAPTER 5

We play possum in the prohibition era

We continue digging up the grammar and piling great heaps of it around the room. Look with pride on what you have done so far. These reeking heaps will soon shoot forth delicate blossoms, miracles of the Latin language.

The great 'I am' again

5a Last chapter we met the irregular verb *sum*, 'I am' (**4e**). More needs to be said about this verb.

(i) When *est* / *sunt* stand first in a sentence, they often mean 'there is/are' e.g. There is a girl … – *est puella* …

(ii) In a two-word sentence *est* often mean 'it is', e.g. *Caesar est* – It's Caesar.

(iii) In 'Delia is a slave', 'Delia' is the subject (so in the nom.) and 'is' is the verb. 'Slave' describes Delia (and is called the *complement*). Since 'Delia' is in the nom., 'slave' will therefore be nom. as well: *Delia serva est*.

So: the verb 'to be' takes a *complement* in the nom.

Exercise

Translate: *Deus Christus est et Christus Deus; Delia est; Camilla serva non est; sunt Harold et Willelmus; quis est Christus?; Normannus es; Deus in* (into) *mundum venit; quid est?; vinum vita est et vita vinum; fortuna stella est; cur servus es?*

Prepositions

5b These are little words like 'towards, into, from, through,

43

against, with' which are 'placed before' (*prae-positus*) nouns. Here we are about to do something enormously cunning.

Observe: *e* (or *ex*) *bello*: out of the war

cum filio: with the son

in aqua: in the water (waving or drowning).

Have we met case-endings in *-o* like *bello* and *filio* yet? No. Who cares? *e* or *ex* means 'out of', *cum* means 'with'. The case endings are in fact the ablative case (as is *aqua* in *in aqua*) but we do not need to worry about that at the moment.

Jolly nice having an early peek at a new case, though.

Other prepositions put the nouns they control in the acc. case. We have met the acc.: no problems.

5c So: **RECORD** the following prepositions:

(i) Followed by the acc.: *ad* towards, near, *in* into, *contra* against, *per* through, *post* after.

E.g. *ad aquam* towards the water, *in aquam* into the water, *contra Anglum* against the Englishman.

(ii) Followed by the abl.: *ex* out of, *in* in, *cum* with.

E.g. *ex aqua* out of the water, *in aqua* actually *in* the water, *cum Christo* with Christ.

There is one hitch: *in* followed by the acc. means 'into'. Followed by the abl., it means 'actually in'. Since you know the acc. case, a little care should solve the problem.

Exercise

Translate: *in palatium, in palatio, in bello, in bellum, in terra, in terram.*

Translate: *post proelium e palatio in locum cum filio venit; eam in proelium per tenebram ducimus; hic Willelmus post bellum Normannum in terram mittit; quis in tenebra est?; servum e terra ad lunam equitare iubent; Haroldus Anglum contra Normannum cum servo mittit; serva prandium ad eum portat; quis in loco cum Anglo est?; per fortunam Haroldum vincimus; post prandium per terram in bellum festinamus; cum Haroldo equitant ad proelium; in principio creat Deus caelum et terram; propter tenebram Normannum non videmus.*

ad aqvam   in aqvam

in aqva   ex aqva

Playing possum

5d *sum* 'I am' occurs in a number of compound forms. The most common is *possum*, I can, am able (to). This combines *pot-* ('able', cf. potential) with *sum*, and conjugates: *pos-sum, pot-es, pot-est, pos-sumus, pot-estis, pos-sunt*, infin. **posse**, to be able. Observe that *t* + *s* becomes *-ss-*.

45

It is followed by the infinitive, e.g. *videre possumus*, we can/are able to see.

Prohibition

5e The Latin for 'don't!' is *noli* (*s*) *nolite* (*pl*). It means literally 'do not want to' and, like *possum*, it too takes the infin. Thus *noli venire* don't come! (*s*), *nolite festinare* don't hurry (*pl*).

Exercise

Translate: *hic locum videre non possunt; noli in aquam post eum venire!; non possum Haroldum iubere vinum portare; nolite per terram equitare!; Diana nunc prandium ministrare potest; nolite pugnare cum servo!; quid facere potest in proelio?; per caelum equitare non potes; noli Normannum post bellum apprehendere.*

Don't (*s*) fight! we cannot hurry; they can ride; don't (*pl*) listen!; they cannot make dinner; you (*s*) cannot see the star; don't (*pl*) announce the battle!

Answers

5a God is Christ and Christ God; it's Delia; Camilla is not a slave; there are Harold and William; who is Christ?; you are a Norman; God comes into the world; what is it?; wine is life and life wine; fortune is a star; why are you a slave?

5c Into the palace, in the palace, in war, into war, in the land, into the land.

After the battle he comes from the palace into the place with his son; we lead her into battle through the shadow; here William after the war sends a Norman into the land; who is in the shadow?; they order the slave to ride from earth to the moon; Harold sends an Englishman against the Norman with a slave; the slave carries dinner to him; who is in the place with the Englishman?; through luck we conquer Harold; after dinner we hurry through the land into war; they ride with Harold to battle; in the beginning God creates heaven and earth

5e Here they cannot see the place; don't come into the water after him; I cannot order Harold to carry the wine; don't ride

46

through the land; Diana can now serve the dinner; don't fight with the slave; what can he do in battle?; you cannot ride through heaven; don't seize the Norman after the war.
noli pugnare; festinare non possumus; equitare possunt; nolite audire; prandium facere non possunt; stellam videre non potes; nolite proelium nuntiare!

The world of Rome

The rape of Lucretia

We have already seen how the rape and suicide of Lucretia caused the Romans, in 509 BC, to revolt from the Etruscan kings who ruled them and establish the Roman republic. The Roman historian Livy (59 BC – AD 17) tells the tale, and a cracker it is.

Sextus, son of king Tarquinius, secretly inflamed with lust for Lucretia, invited himself as a trusted guest to her home while her husband was away on military service. Greeted with all civility and given a bed for the night, when it was quiet he crept into her bedroom, drew his sword and, threatening to kill her if she made any noise, attempted to persuade her to yield to him. She refused. When he then said he would murder her, cut a slave's throat, lay the slave beside her and claim he had caught them in the act, Lucretia yielded.

Next day she informed her husband and father, proclaiming that her body had been violated, but her heart was innocent, and she would prove it by committing suicide. They begged her not to. She was innocent, they said: without intention, there could never be guilt. In vain: she drew a knife, stabbed herself and fell dead.

This story, and the whole issue of martyrdom, greatly interested later Christian thinkers. St Jerome admired women who killed themselves for the sake of their chastity: they were early examples of virtuous (if heathen) martyrs. St Augustine, however, argued that chastity was a matter of the will, not of the body, and should not be over-valued for its own sake; further, suicide was self-murder and therefore always wrong.

Word play

We have already met *duco*, 'I lead'. Its stems (*duc-* and, as we shall find out later, *duct-*) have flourished in English. By the addition of prefixes (elements fixed at the front, often prepositions) and suffixes (elements fixed at the back) Latin generated abduct, abduction (*ab* 'away from'); adduce, adduct (*ad* 'towards'); aqueduct (*aqua* 'water'); conduce, conduct, conductor (con- = *cum*, 'with'); deduce, deduct (*de* 'down/away from'); educe (*e(x)* 'out of '); induce, induct, induction (*in* 'into'); introduce (*intro* 'inside'); produce, product, producer, production (*pro* 'forward, in front'); reduce (*re* 'back, again'); reproduce; and so on.

One can play the same games endlessly: consider, for example, *porto* 'carry' and *re-, im-, ex-, trans-, de-, com-, sub-* (= sup- 'under'), and so on. In this context, people often complain about the formation of hybrid words – combinations of Latin and some other language (e.g. television – *tele* being Greek, 'afar' and vision from Latin *video* 'I see'). But hybrid formations are ten a penny. Consider, for example the frequency with which the Latin suffix -ible/able (*-ibilis, -abilis*) is routinely attached to Anglo-Saxon stems (e.g. bearable, readable, gullible); or the Greek suffix -ist (*-istes*) is attached to Latin stems (scientist, artist, linguist – indeed, even classicist and purist!). Words in everyday use like automobile, monocle, heterosexual, petrol, bicycle, prehistory and criminology happily combine Greek and Latin stems, without touching a nerve.

CHAPTER 6

We decline for the third time

As you may already have observed, there is a long and healthy tradition of daft sentences in Latin courses. The whole point of a daft sentence is that its meaning cannot be anticipated. It forces you to pay close attention to the Latin.

The world of many Latin courses is dominated by surreal, Dali-esque scenarios involving kings and moons and virgins and Angles. We are practising our grammar. If the Latin is correct, that (for the moment) is sufficient. Besides, it make such a nice surprise when someone says something sensible.

Enjoy this lunacy while you can. Grim reality will, alas, soon enough rear its terrible head in the next chapter, when we take on the Bayeux tapestry, and the chapter after that, with our first love song.

3rd decl. nouns

6a So far we have met nouns of the 1st decl. f. (like *serva*) and the 2nd decl. m. (like *servus*) and n. (like *bellum*).

Eyes down, then, for the 3rd decl.

Submit the following sentences to an intensive scrutiny, faculties humming:

dux Haroldum mittit: the general sends Harold
Haroldus ducem mittit: Harold sends the general
miles servum portat: the soldier carries the slave
servus militem portat: the slave carries the soldier
navis ad terram venit: the ship comes towards the land
navem video: I see the ship

6b It is at once apparent that *dux* general, *miles* soldier and

navis ship (the nom. forms) all have different endings (*-x, -es, -is*) in the nom. But in the acc., something happens to these nom. forms (*dux* becomes *duc-*, *miles* becomes *milit-*, and *navis* becomes *nav-*). Further, onto all of them the common ending *-em* is then attached to form the acc. (*duc-em, milit-em, nav-em*). What is going on?

Changing the stem

6c Here is another very important principle – that of the changing stem. The nom. form of 'general' is *dux*, but the stem is *duc-*; of 'soldier' it is *miles*, but the stem is *milit-*; and so on. This is a bit of a monster. The fact is that there is no way of being certain what the stem of any 3rd decl. noun is. You just have to

50

learn it. But we are Latinists. We like discipline and knowing things. No wishy-washy guesswork for us.

The important point to remember is that 3rd decl. nouns all exhibit this feature. So when you record 3rd decl. nouns, you must record both the nom. and the stem. While watching your endings, therefore, remember at the same time to take a firm grip on your stem.

RECORD *amor amor-*, n. 3m love (note connection with *amo*, I love); *dux duc-*, n. 3m leader, general, duke (note connection with *duco*, I lead); *homo homin-*, n. 3m man, fellow; *miles milit-*, n. 3m soldier; *mater matr-*, n. 3f mother; *mulier mulier-*, n. 3f wife, woman; *navis nav-*, n. 3f ship; *pater patr-*, n. 3m father; *rex reg-*, n. 3m king (compare *rego*, I rule); *virgo virgin-*, n. 3f young girl.

As you can see, in the third decl. there is a huge number of nom. endings (e.g. just in the list above, *-or*, *-ux*, *-o*, *-es*, *-er*, *-is*, *-ex*). Don't worry about that. The vital thing is to know the stem. The stem appears as the basis of all the other cases. So it is, in fact, far more common than the nom. .

You will also note that there is no rule about which nouns are masculine and which feminine: *homo*, for example, is m., while *virgo* is f.; *pater* is m., but *mulier* is f., and so on. Here again, you just have to learn them. Take heart from the fact that, for translation purposes at the moment, the gender of the noun is not important.

Note the connections between the vocabulary list and English.

Exercise

1. Get the right stem and form the acc. of *rex, virgo, aqua, mulier, servus, miles, mundus, pater, deus, homo, bellum, amor, vinum.*

2. What is the nom. of *hominem, proelium, militem, locum, navem, tenebram, matrem, vitam, virginem, angelum, ducem?*

3. Translate: *navem mittimus; mulierem vident; hic rex ducem regit, hic dux militem ducit; amor omnia* (everything, acc.) *vincit; quid homo nunc facit?; virgo hominem amare non potest; mater patrem in navem mittit; Normannus militem virginem capere iubet; e palatio rex venit cum milite* (s); *nolite in*

navem festinare!; dux regem e loco (s) *per aquam in palatium cum servo* (s) *mittit; equum* (horse, acc.) *ad aquam ducere potes, sed ....*

4. Translate: the soldier loves the slave-girl; the king sends the fellow into the palace; the general comes towards the ship; father and mother hurry into the palace; why does the fellow not know?; what does the young girl feel? the woman sees him but not her.

N.b. (=*nota bene*, note well): if you have a preference for English-into-Latin or Latin-into-English, you can use the **Answers** as the exercise and check your answers against the exercise.

Answers

6c 1. *regem, virginem, aquam, mulierem, servum, militem, mundum, patrem, deum, hominem, bellum, amorem, vinum.*

2. *homo, proelium, miles, locus, navis, tenebra, mater, vita, virgo, angelus, dux.*

3. We send the ship; they see the woman; here the king rules the general, here the general leads the soldier; love conquers everything; what is the fellow doing now? the young girl cannot love the fellow; mother sends father into the ship; the Norman orders the soldier to capture the young girl; the king comes from the palace with the soldier; don't (*pl*) hurry into the ship!; the general sends the king from the place through the water into the palace with the servant; you can lead a horse to the water but ....

4. *miles servam amat; rex hominem in palatium mittit; dux ad navem venit; pater et mater in palatium festinant; cur homo nescit?; quid virgo sentit? mulier eum videt, sed non eam.*

The world of Rome

The treacherous schoolmaster

In 509 BC Rome threw out the Etruscan kings who had ruled it for over 200 years. It then began to flex its muscles. It took on its neighbours one by one and expanded its power throughout Italy till in 295 BC the whole Italian peninsula was under its control. Livy, the historian of early Rome, embroiders the story with many an improving tale.

In the siege of the town of Falerii in 390 BC, the Roman general Camillus was finding things hard going. A stroke of luck gave him the town. The children of the leaders of Falerii were taught, Livy tells us, by the best available scholar. He was in the habit of taking them for play and exercise outside the city walls even during the siege, and gradually he extended these expeditions till one day he took his young charges through the Roman outposts and right into Camillus' headquarters. 'These boys' parents', he said to Camillus, 'run Falerii. I have delivered them to you. Falerii is yours.'

Camillus was outraged. 'We may be at war, but war has its laws as peace does, and we are bound by bonds of common humanity. We are fighting men, not children.' He stripped the master, gave the boys sticks, and told them to beat him all the way back into Falerii. Overwhelmed by this display of Roman honour and justice, the people of Falerii capitulated at once.

It was this sort of behaviour that historians like the Greek Polybius (c. 220-118 BC) found so admirable in Romans. In particular, Polybius argued that the key to Rome's success was the frequency and solemnity with which it practised its public religious rituals – not because this made the gods favour it, but because it kept their officials (who worked under oath) on the straight and narrow, and the masses in awe and under control.

Word play

In the last chapter, we saw how easy it was to generate a huge number of words by playing with prefixes, stems and suffixes, and how many quite innocent hybrid words were thrown up in this way. Concern for the 'purity' of the language has been with us for some time, however. For example, Latin *debitum* ('something owed') developed in French into *dette*. English scholars were shocked by this, so insisted on writing it 'debt', to signify more clearly the (cough) debt to Latin. Doubt is a similar instance – Latin *dubito*, French *doute*, English doubt (in *Love's Labour's Lost* V.i, Shakespeare has some fun with pedants who insist that the 'b' in such words be pronounced).

Likewise, Latin *advenio* yielded French *aventure*, to which we added 'd' to turn it into adventure. On the same principle, we turned French *avancer* into advance – this time, wrongly. Scholars did not know that *avancer* derived from vulgar (=everyday) Latin *abantiare*. The word should therefore have been 'corrected' to abvance, or perhaps even abance.

CHAPTER 7

We learn to take our orders

Six chapters have passed, and we are now getting ready for the real thing. In this chapter, we shake a tentative stick at the Bayeux tapestry. Next chapter, we go all soppy over a love-song from the 13th century AD *Carmina Burana* (one of those poems set to music by Carl Orff in 1937). St Jerome's 4th century Vulgate (*vulgata editio*, people's edition) of the Bible is not far off.

Get fell in!

7a You can already say 'don't do X!' in Latin (*noli* (s), *nolite* (pl) + infin., **5e**).

But how do you say 'do X'? Very easily. Cooks say it all the time – *recipe* is Latin for 'take!'. N.b. is *nota bene*, 'note well', *dona nobis pacem* means 'grant us peace', *festina lente* 'hurry slowly'. A *vade mecum* is a 'come with me'. And everyone knows the injunction *cave canem* – 'beware of the dog'.

Here, then, are the *s* and *pl* imperative (*impero*, 'I order') forms enabling you to say 'do X!'. As you will see, they consist of verb stem + key vowel (*s*), and verb-stem + key vowel + *-te* (*pl*).

Use the *s* when you are addressing just one person.

1st conj. *ama, ama-te!* 'love!'; 2nd conj. *mone, mone-te* 'warn!'; 3rd conj. *rege, reg-ite* 'rule!'; 4th conj. *audi, audi-te* 'listen!'; 5th conj. *cape, cap-ite* 'capture!'

Notate bene: (i) the irregular imperatives *dic, dicite* 'speak!', *duc, ducite* 'lead!' and *fac, facite* 'do, make!'. Cue hoary mnemonic '*Dic* had a *duc* and that's a *fac*'.

(ii) the useful idioms *salve, salvete*, and *ave, avete* 'welcome! hail!' and *vale, valete*, 'farewell! good bye!'

FESTINA LENTE

CAVE CANEM

Exercise

Translate: *venite e palatio et audite!; festina in locum, homo!; ama, noli pugnare!; vale, Diana, salve, Camilla; nolite virginem capere, sed militem apprehendite! homo, duc equum* (horse, acc.) *ad aquam; dic, rex, et audi, dux; festinatis lente* (slowly) *contra hominem; amate Deum; portatis vinum et aquam ad navem; nota bene; prandium fac; rex, sapienter* (wisely) *rege, dux, fortiter* (bravely) *duc; duc me* (me) *ad vestrum* (your) *ducem.*

Here is Catullus' haunting farewell to his dead brother (*frater*):

atque (and) *in perpetuum, frater, ave atque vale.*

Here is a line of bogus Latin poetry:

iamque (now), *Diana, vale; salve, regina* (queen) *Camilla.*

Plurals

7b So far we have used nouns only in the singular (*s*). But they have plurals (*pl*) too. Observe the following and draw your conclusions:

1st declension f., like *serva* (acc. *servam*)
serv-ae serv-as amant '(female) slaves love (female) slaves'

2nd declension m., like *servus* (acc. *servum*)
serv-i serv-os amant '(male) slaves love (male) slaves'

2nd declension n., like *bellum* (acc. *bellum*)
bell-a bell-a faciunt 'wars make wars'

3rd declension, like *miles* (acc. *militem*)
duc-es duc-es amant 'leaders love leaders'

Deeply difficult. We can thus categorise as follows:

1st declension (f.)
Singular
nom.	*serv-a*
acc.	*serv-am*

Plural
nom.	*serv-ae*
acc.	*serv-as*

2nd declension (m.)
Singular
nom.	*serv-us*
acc.	*serv-um*

Plural
nom.	*serv-i*
acc.	*serv-os*

2nd declension (n.)
Singular
nom.	*bell-um*
acc.	*bell-um*

Plural
nom.	*bell-a*
acc.	*bell-a*

3rd declension (m., f.)
Singular
nom.	*dux*
acc.	*duc-em*

Plural

nom.   *duc-es*

acc.   *duc-es*

Note: acc. *pl* of *eum* 'him' = *eos* 'them'; of *eam* 'her' = *eas* 'them'.

1st and 2nd decl. cause no problem, but note 3rd decl., where nom. and acc. *pl* forms are the same, i.e. stem + *-es*. Thus the sentence *duces reges amant* could mean 'leaders love kings' or 'kings love leaders'. We have met this problem already with 2nd decl. n. nouns like *bellum*, so it is not new. As usual, only the context will supply the right answer: *mulieres naves portant* – the women carry the ships? *virgines milites vincunt* – the girls defeat the soldiers?

Exercise

1. Form the plural, depending what the given *s* form is: thus *mundus* (nom. *s*) has the *pl mundi* (nom. *pl*), *mundum* (acc. *s*) the *pl mundos* (acc. *pl*), etc.

Remember: get the right stem on to which to put the right endings. Each noun type will have its own stem and its own endings – each type stays true to type. See *Grammatical Summary* 124-131 for stems and endings (but remember 3rd decl. stems are not predictable).

servus, hominem, angelum, eum, vinum, deum, dux, prandium, regem.

2. Turn these *pl* to *s*: *loci, principia, duces* (two options), *stellas, proelia, eas, reges* (two options), *deos, stellae.*

Bayeux Tapestry

These sentences come from the Bayeux tapestry. Note (i) alternative spellings of e.g. William, (ii) absence of *-us* in some proper names in the nom., (iii) *hic* 'here', to indicate what is happening on the tapestry:

Harold(us) dux et milites equitant ad Bosham ('Bosham'); *hic dux Wilgelm(us) cum Haroldo venit ad palatium; hic milites pugnant contra Dinantes* ('men of Dinan'); *hic Harold(us) dux reversus est* (='returned') *ad Anglicam terram et venit ad Edwar-*

dum regem; hic Willelm(us) dux venit ad Pevenesae (= Pevensey); *hic milites ad pr(o)elium veniunt; hic est dux Wilelmus; hic
Franci pugnant; hic ceciderunt* ('fell') *Angli et Franci in pr(o)elio.*

Answers

7a Come from the palace and listen; hurry into the place, man;
make love, not war; farewell, Diana, welcome, Camilla; do not
take the girl, but arrest the soldier; fellow, lead the horse to the
water; speak, king, and listen, leader; you are hurrying slowly
against the man; love God; you are carrying wine and water to
the ship; note well; make dinner; king, rule wisely, leader, lead
bravely; take me to your leader; and for ever, brother, hail and
farewell; now Diana, farewell, welcome, queen Camilla.
7c 1. *servi, homines, angelos, eos, vina, deos, duces, prandia,
reges*.

2. *locus, principium, dux/ducem, stellam, proelium, eam,
rex/regem, deum, stella*.

3. Duke Harold and the soldiers ride to Bosham; here Duke
William comes with Harold to the palace; here soldiers fight
against the men of Dinan; here Duke Harold returned to English
soil and comes to King Edward; here Duke William comes to
Pevensey; here soldiers come to battle; here is Duke William;
here the Franks fight; here the English and Franks fell in battle.

The world of Rome

Hannibal crosses the Alps

The Carthaginians had settled in North Africa (modern Tunis)
from Phoenicia (Lebanon) in the ninth century BC under the
legendary Queen Dido (*Carthago* is the Roman formation of the
semitic Qart Hadasht, 'New City'). Phoenicia was a very great
trading nation indeed with a scintillating culture, and sent
colonies all over the western Mediterranean, especially to Spain,
and traded in tin as far as Britain.

Carthaginians first clashed with the growing might of Rome
in 262 BC over the control of Sicily (first Punic war: *Punici* is the
Latinised form of *Phoinikes*), but lost. Sicily, Sardinia and Cor-
sica at once became the first Roman provinces – the empire had
begun.

They clashed again in 218 BC over control of Spain, and this time their leader Hannibal (the Latinised form of Chenu Baal, 'Grace of Baal') pre-empted the Romans with an astonishing dash through Spain and southern France, over the Alps and down into Italy itself, elephants and all. Some crushing victories (Lake Trasimene, Cannae) brought Hannibal to Rome's gates and Rome almost to its knees but Hannibal could not strike the decisive blow. Rome slowly recovered, took the battle back to Spain and (in 205 BC) into Africa itself. Hannibal was recalled in 203 BC and in 202 BC was defeated by Scipio 'the thunderbolt' at Zama.

The key to Rome's power was its pure determination – it never offered Hannibal peace terms, even when he was at the gates of Rome – and its ability to mobilise huge citizen armies. From now on, Rome kept up its military strength on a scale unmatched anywhere else in the Mediterranean. It was no longer just another city-state, but a growing power, and it proved it by punishing places which had supported Hannibal.

Rome began with King Philip of Macedon (Greece), and by 146 BC Greece too had become a province. This was to prove a crucial moment in European history. The Romans were bowled over by the brilliance of Greek culture and set about both preserving it, absorbing it and creatively adapting it. Without that Roman 'takeover', it is very hard to say how much of an ancient Greek heritage we would today be enjoying.

Word play

In the last chapter, we saw how the spelling of some French words was changed when they were taken over into English in order to reflect more closely their Latin origins (or what were regarded, sometimes wrongly, as their Latin origins). In fact, until the 18th century, the spelling of English was in a chaotic state – Anglo-Saxon, French and Graeco-Latin patterns had all been adopted over the centuries, with no consistency at all.

For most people, this simply did not matter. Everyone knows Shakespeare spelled his name in many different ways, and we have already seen that the Bayeux tapestry spells 'William' inconsistently too. Concern, however, began to be expressed as early as the 16th century, but until grammars and dictionaries began to be produced, consistency and conformity were impossible dreams – for where was the authority to impose them?

In the 18th century, scholars began to address the issue. Their aim was to codify the language and try to show that there was method in its (apparent) madness; to provide ways of settling disputes; and to point out 'errors'. Thus began the great debate, still with us today – should we attempt to *prescribe* how language works, establishing rules for grammar and spelling, or should we merely *describe* common usage? As far as spelling goes, prescription seems to be winning the day, and this is surely right: as English becomes a universal language, written communication at any rate would be almost impossible unless conventions of spelling were universally agreed.

CHAPTER 8

We discover pure perfection

8a So far we have been living in the present, with verbs of present tense, e.g. *rego* 'I rule'. This will not do. We are Latinists. The past is our country. So this week, with a sigh of relief, we decamp there. Welcome, then, the perfect tense, and a special round of applause for our old chums from the Seven Dwarfs, *ven-i, vid-i* and *vic-i* – perfects to a man.

The perfect tense 'I (have) -ed'

8b Take *rego*. We have so far learned two of its main forms – *rego* 'I rule' and the infin. *regere* 'to rule'. These are its first two so-called 'principal parts' (p.p.). The perfect form is its third p.p. Eyes down: *rex-i.*

Analysis: *rex-* is the perfect stem. The ending *-i* is the first person ending. *rexi* therefore means 'I ruled' or 'I have ruled' or 'I did rule'. Here *rexi* is conjugated in full:

1s	*rex-i*	'I (have) ruled, did rule'
2s	*rex-isti*	'you (*s*) (have) ruled, did rule'
3s	*rex-it*	'he/she/it (has) ruled, did rule'
1pl	*rex-imus*	'we ruled (have) ruled, did rule'
2pl	*rex-istis*	'you (*pl*) (have) ruled, did rule'
3pl	*rex-erunt*	'they (have) ruled, did rule'

Observe the person endings: *-i, -isti, -it, -imus, -istis, -erunt.* Note our old friends *-t* (3 *s*), *-mus* (1 *pl*), *-tis* (2 *pl*) and *-nt* (3 *pl*). As you will discover, these endings apply to all perfects across all five conjugations. Good, regular language, Latin.

Stem-change

8c As you can see, the 3rd p.p. has a different stem from the 1st p.p.: *reg-* of the present becomes *rex-* in the perfect.

Do you then form the perfect stem by adding *-s-i* to the present stem (*reg-s-i = rex-i*)? After all, you will soon see the perfect stem of *dic-o* is *dix-i* and of *duc-o* is *dux-i*.

Alas, no. Rather as we saw with 3rd decl. nouns (see **6c**), stem changes can be violent and unpredictable. Regretfully, one must point out that the perfect stem in many cases cannot be predicted. It just has to be known. But there is some good news to tell, when you have finished **8d** and its exercise.

Some perfect forms

8d RECORD now the following perfect forms. The first two principal parts are given as well for revision purposes:

apprehend-o 3v apprehend-ere **apprehend-i** 'I seized'; *cap-io 5v cap-ere* **cep-i** 'I caught'; *dic-o 3v dic-ere* **dix-i** 'I said'; *duc-o 3v duc-ere* **dux-i** 'I led'; *fac-io 5v fac-ere* **fec-i** 'I did, made'; *iube-o 3v iube-re* **iuss-i** 'I ordered'; *mitt-o 3v mitt-ere* **mis-i** 'I sent'; *senti-o 4v senti-re* **sens-i** 'I felt'; *veni-o 4v veni-re* **ven-i** 'I came'; *vide-o 3v vide-re* **vid-i** 'I saw'; *vinc-o 3v vinc-ere* **vic-i** 'I conquered'.

sum 'I am', as usual, goes seriously bananas: *sum, esse* **fu-i** 'I was, I have been'. So *possum* 'I can' *posse* **potu-i** 'I could, was able, have been able'.

Exercise

Remember: get the right stem. Perfect tense requires perfect stem and perfect endings.

1. Form the 3rd (*s*) and 3rd (*pl*) perfect of: *capio, dico, duco, sum, mitto, facio, video, venio*.

2. Turn the following present forms into their perfect equivalent, and translate e.g. *dicis* ('you say') becomes *dixisti* ('you said'), etc. You will, of course, need to know the perfect stem in order to do this:

apprehenditis, capit, sunt, dicimus, possunt, ducunt, facis, est, iubes, mitto, sentimus, veniunt, vides, sumus, vincitis.

3. Translate: he came, he saw, he conquered; we have caught; she was; you (*s*) felt; they ordered; she has sent; you (*s*) led; they were able; I seized; you (*pl*) have been; we made.

The good news is that we have done the difficult bit first. Most of the verbs we have looked at above are 3rd and 5th conj., and their perfect stem is always unpredictable and has to be known. These verbs are also very common indeed – which is why we are tucking them under our belts now.

But the perfect stem of most 1st, 2nd and 4th conj. verbs is regularly formed. We shall come to them in **Chapter 12**. Meanwhile, get a firm grip on these 3rd and 5th conj. perfect stems.

Bayeux tapestry

8e Translate: *hic Willelm dux iussit milites naves* (*a*)*edificare* (*aedifico* 1v build); *hic trahunt naves ad mare* (sea); *hic milites portant armas* (guess!) *ad naves, et hic trahunt carrum* (cart) *cum vino et armis; hic milites venerunt ad pr(o)elium contra Haroldum regem.*

Vocatives

8f The vocative case is used when you address someone, e.g. '*Trevor*, bend over', '*Donald*, what are you doing?'

As a matter of fact, you have been using it all the way through the course and never noticed. That is because the vocative is the same form as the nom.

There is one major exception: 2nd decl. nouns like *servus* have a voc. s. in -*e*, e.g. 'o slave' (*o*) *serve* (but the *pl* follows the rule:'o slaves' is *o servi*, just like the nom *pl*).

Exercise

Translate: *Angle, quid fecisti?; ave et vale; Harolde, noli venire contra militem; post prandium equitare non potui, Willelme dux; milites, date prandium; noli me tangere* (touch); *dic, dux; fac, rex; audite, servi; salvete, angeli.*

65

Carmina Burana (13th century AD)

8g Note the following vocabulary (in order of occurrence): *tempus* time; *iocundum* joyful; *modo* now; *congaude-o* rejoice together; *vos* you; *iuven-is* young man; *totus* all over; *flore-o* I flower, flourish; *iam* now; *amore virginali* with pure love; *arde-o* I burn; *novus* fresh, new; *quo* by which; *pere-o* I perish; *domicella* darling; *gaudi-um* joy; *pulchra* my beauty.

> *tempus est iocundum*
> *o virgines,*
> *modo congaudete,*
> *vos iuvenes.*
>
> *o, o,*
> *totus floreo,*
> *iam amore virginali*
> *totus ardeo,*
> *novus, novus amor*
> *est, quo pereo.*

veni, domicella,
cum gaudio,
veni, veni, pulchra,
iam pereo.

Answers

8d 1. *cepit ceperunt, dixit dixerunt, duxit duxerunt, fuit fuerunt, misit miserunt, fecit fecerunt, vidit viderunt, venit venerunt.*

2. *apprehendistis, cepit, fuerunt, diximus, potuerunt, duxerunt, fecisti, fuit, iussisti, misi, sensimus, venerunt, vidisti, fuimus, vicistis.*

3. *venit, vidit, vicit; cepimus; fuit; sensisti; iusserunt; misit; duxisti; potuerunt; apprehendi; fuistis; fecimus.*

8e Here Duke William ordered soldiers to build ships; here they drag ships to the sea; here soldiers carry weapons to the ships, and here they drag a cart with wine and weapons; here soldiers came to battle against Harold the king.

8f Englishman, what did you do?; hail and farewell; Harold, do not come against the soldier; after lunch I could not ride, Duke William; soldiers, give lunch; do no touch me; speak, leader; do, king; listen, slaves; welcome, angels.

8g The time is joyful, young girls; now rejoice together, you young men; O, o, I flower all over, now with pure love all over I burn; new, new is the love of which I die. Come, darling, with joy, come come, (my) beauty, now I die.

The world of Rome

The grandest old Roman

Marcus Porcius Cato (234-149 BC, Cato 'the Elder') lived during the critical period when Rome, having defeated Hannibal, was poised to become the greatest power in the Mediterranean. The prospect filled him with excitement and foreboding. A stern moralist, who applauded a young aristocrat coming out of a reeking brothel because it kept adultery down, he raised issues of integrity in government, the duties of a world power, the obligations of the wealthy, and cultural integrity.

He was, for example, deeply suspicious of Greek culture. In a letter to his son, he says 'It is a good idea to dip into their literature, but not to develop a thorough acquaintance. Greeks are a most iniquitious and intractable people, and you may take my word as the word of a prophet: if that people shall ever bestow their literature on us, it will ruin everything'. But he eventually yielded and learnt Greek himself, as all cultured Romans did.

Cato set about reforming the lax morals (as he saw it) of the Roman aristocracy, supported a law which limited women's finery, and urged a return to the simple life of the farmer (his 'On agriculture' urges farmers to store crops and sell at a good price not for sordid gain, but for virtue (*virtus*) and fame (*gloria*)). His *Dicta Catonis* ('Sayings of Cato') became standard educational works: they include gems like 'sex and wine cause trouble and pleasure: take the pleasure, avoid the trouble'. Most famously, it was he who demanded that Carthage be finally destroyed (*Carthago delenda est*), as it was in 146 BC (though it was later resurrected as the capital of the Roman province of Africa).

Word play

The introduction of the perfect tense raises a fascinating question about what verbs are able to express. We have already seen that Latin *amo* in the present tense covers no less than three possible meanings in English – 'I love', 'I do love' and 'I am loving'. The first English usage seems to be a plain statement of fact; the second is more assertive; and the third suggests a continuing process. So the idea of 'love' expressed in the present tense in English is given what are called different 'aspects', or 'ways of looking' at the action. The speaker chooses the way the speaker wants to look at it.

Now consider the Latin perfect tense. In English, it is again given three meanings: to take *amavi* as an example, 'I loved', 'I have loved' and 'I did love'. The three forms again offer different 'aspects' of loving in the past. 'I loved' anchors the action firmly in the past, and seems to make a simple statement of fact; 'I did love' asserts it more strongly; but 'I have loved' changes the 'aspect' of loving in the past by somehow drawing it from the past and bringing it up into the present. 'I loved you for ten years' suggests that that love is over, stranded in the past. 'I have loved you for ten years' brings that love more into the present. 'What is the speaker trying to put across by saying things in this way?' is the question to ask.

But where, you may ask, is the idea of a continuing love in the past, to correspond with the continuing 'I am loving' in the present? That job will be done by the imperfect tense, which you will meet in **Chapter 11**.

CHAPTER 9

We get all personal

9a For the past eight chapters we have been living on the edge of a great mystery. We can say 'I love' in Latin without using a word for 'I': *amo* is the answer. Why do the Romans have no words for 'I' or 'you' or 'we' (personal pronouns, as we call them)? What have they got against them?

Nothing, actually. Romans just do not need to use them when they are the subject of a verb. But they do have them, and here they are – with an elegant spin, what's more: we shall present them with a brand new case – not the nom., not the acc., but the dative (dat.).

Taking therefore a large helping of fish and carrots to ensure the cerebral and ocular functions are ticking over with Aristotelian keenness (*cerebrum* 'brain', *oculus* 'eye'), catch an eyeful of this lot:

Personal pronouns

9b *ego te amo, tu me vitas* (*vito* 1 'avoid'): *I* love you, *you* avoid me.

Conclusion? *ego* 'I' nom.; *me* 'me' acc.; *tu* 'you' (*s*) nom., *te* 'you' (*s*) acc.

How delightfully Freudian (ego and that lot), and French (tu, te).

nos vos amamus; vos nos vitatis: we love you (*pl*), *you* (*pl*) avoid us.

Conclusion? *nos* 'we' nom. and *nos* 'us' acc.; *vos* 'you' (*pl*) nom., and *vos* 'you' (*pl*) acc. Compare French nous, vous.

In summary then: *ego me, nos nos: tu te, vos vos.*

nos vos amamus; vos nos vitatis

nos servi sumus, vos milites estis

Personal contrast

Two truths are told as happy prologues to the swelling act of the grammatical theme.

(i) English, like Latin, also has forms that are inflected, i.e. change – 'we' and 'I' subject, but 'me' and 'us' object.

(ii) Latin uses *ego, tu, nos, vos* (in the nom.) usually when it wants to create a strong contrast: '*I* am king, but *you* are general' – ego *rex sum*, tu *dux es*. nos *servi sumus*, vos *milites estis* '*we* are slaves, *you* are soldiers'.

We should also note that *nos*, like *vos*, can be subject or object. Only the context will tell – and especially the verb. After all, if the subject is *nos*, the verb will be 1 *pl*; if the subject is *vos*, it will be 2*pl*. Thus *nos vos amatis* can mean only '*You* love *us*', while *vos nos mittimus* can mean only '*we* send *you*'.

Exercise

Translate: *nos te amamus, tu nos vitas; tu dicis, nos audimus; nos venimus, vos vicistis; tu deus es, ego servus; cur nos misisti?; nunc vos non amo; Haroldus me et te ad palatium venire iussit;*

nos e loco duxerunt; laudamus te (laudo 1, praise), *adoramus te, glorificamus te* (guess!); *ego te cepi, tu me vici; Willelmus nos apprehendere non potuit.*

I ordered, *you (pl)* came; *we* saw you *(s)*, *you* did not see us; *you (s)*, farewell, *you* (all) welcome; *I* was a soldier, *you* the leader; *I'*m warning you, *you* listen!

The dative case

9c By this time you are asking 'And what about this dative case thingy, then, squire? We have enjoyed your exposition of our old friends the nom. and acc., but we are hungry for more. Hit us with the dat., and be quick about it.'

Well, you said it, not me. Here goes. Mark, learn and inwardly digest:

ego tibi dico, tu mihi non respondes (**RECORD** *respondeo* 2v *respondere respondi* 'reply'): I speak *to you*, you do not reply *to me*.

nos vobis diximus, vos nobis non respondistis: we spoke *to you (pl)*, you did not reply *to us*.

9d So! The dative case means 'to' (or 'for'), not in the sense of motion (that is *ad* or *in* + acc.) but in the sense of being on the receiving end, as an interested party. It is most common with words of speaking ('X said *to me*', *mihi*) and giving ('X gives this *to us*', *nobis*). That is why it is called the dative, from Latin *do* 'I give'.

So we can now add to our little declension: *ego me mihi, tu te tibi; nos nos nobis, vos vos vobis*. See *Grammatical Summary* 129, 130.

While we are about it, let us throw in the dat. of *eum / eam: ei* 'to him/her' *(s)*, *eis* 'to them' *(pl)*.

Exercise

Translate: *Iesus ei dixit; nobis responderunt; dic nobis, rex; quid mihi dant?; tu nobis prandium das, nos tibi vinum; quid eis dixisti, dux?; cur vobis non respondimus?; cur vobis non respondemus?; noli eis equum mittere!; mater non mihi sed tibi respondit; da mihi vinum, serve, da ei nihil* (nothing); *non nobis, domine* (Lord), *sed tibi sit* (be) *gloria.*

Martial

9e The satirist Martial (AD 40-104) wrote this poem to Sabidius (vocative *Sabidi*):

non amo te, Sabidi, nec (nor) *possum dicere quare* (why):
   hoc tantum (this alone) *possum dicere, non amo te.*

Compare: 'I do not love thee, Dr Fell ...'.

Answers

9b We love you, you avoid us; you speak, we listen; we came, you conquered; you are a god, I a slave; why did you send us? now I do not love you; Harold ordered me and you to come to the palace; they led us from the place; we praise you, we adore you, we glorify you; I captured you, you conquered me; William could not take us.
ego iussi, vos venistis; nos te vidimus, tu nos non vidisti; tu vale, vos salvete; ego miles fui, tu dux; ego te moneo, tu audi!
9d Jesus said to him/her; they replied to us; speak to us, king; what do they give to me?; you are giving (to) us dinner, we (give) (to) you wine; what did you say to them, leader?; why did we not reply to you? why do we not reply to you; do not send (to) them a horse!; mother replied not to me but to you; give (to) me wine, slave, give (to) him nothing; not unto us, Lord, but unto thee be the glory.
9e I do not love you, Sabidius, nor can I say why. This alone I can say, I do not love you.

The world of Rome

The Ides of March

Julius Caesar was assassinated on March 15 44 BC. His dying words were not, in fact, *et tu, Brute* but Greek: *kai su* (you), *teknon* ('you too, child'). Some in Rome did indeed think that Caesar, who had had a passionate affair with Brutus' mother, was father of Brutus, but even if that is not the case (and it almost certainly is not), Caesar's words are still barbed: not a cry of anguish but a vicious retort, meaning 'and the same to you' (with, as it were, knives in).

Caesar was killed because Rome was not ready for him. The republican system was in fact at an end. Ambitious dynasts like Pompey and Caesar with armies at their back had ridden rough-shod over rule by the Senate, and after winning the civil war against Pompey, Caesar was now uncrowned king. But as Cicero said in a letter written just before the war, 'What we see now is a struggle for personal power at the state's peril'.

Cicero was right. Caesar was, of course, aware of the danger of his position. He became renowned for his mildness and gen-erosity to political enemies. But forgiveness was the prerogative of a tyrant. Republican idealists like Brutus resented the idea that their careers depended on an individual's whim. So they killed him. It would take nearly fifteen more years of civil war for Romans to realise the truth and be ready to accept the idea of an emperor – in the person of Caesar's adopted son and heir, Octavian, soon to take on the title Augustus.

Word play

The real difficulty with Latin lies in the case-endings and the word-order. Whereas in English, word-order and prepositions carry the grammatical meaning ('Caesar (subject) gives (verb) a lion (object) to (preposition) Jenny'), case-ending is the main bearer of grammatical meaning in Latin, and the words can come in (almost) any order. 'Gives Jenny lion Caesar' is a perfectly respectable Latin word-order, that would mean exactly the same as the English above if 'Caesar' were in the nom., 'lion' in the acc., and 'Jenny' in the dat.

Yet there is a residual case-system in English. We have met it in this chapter, in the changing forms of 'we' (subject) and 'us' (all other cases). Consider further, for example, 'he/him/his', 'she/her/her(s)', 'it, its', 'they/them/their(s)'. Yet yokels are al-lowed to burble 'Aaargh, him loves she', and we understand perfectly well what the yokel means because the word-order tells us that 'him' is the subject and 'she' the object. Word-order in English, in other words, usually overrides case.

Some poets have used Latinate word order for special effect. Try the following line of poetry by Alexander Pope (18th century), analysing as you go along: 'Pleasures' – probably subject; could be verb?; 'the' – hmm?; 'sex' – gosh; 'as' – I am getting lost; 'children' – ??? call the Child Abuse hot-line; 'birds' – what *is* going on?; 'pursue' – thank heavens, a certain verb at last, but what is the subject, what the object? Answer 'The sex [Pope means women] pursue pleasures as children (pursue) birds'. Crunchy stuff.

CHAPTER 10

We lay the dative to rest

10a In the last chapter we met personal pronouns and a new case, the dative (dat.). It meant 'to' (or 'for'), not in the sense of movement, but in the sense of being on the receiving end of something, as an interested party. It was used especially with verbs of giving, offering, showing and speaking to someone.

So far, we can say only 'to me, to you, to us, to him/her/them'. Exciting though that undoubtedly is, you will now be yearning to know what form the dative takes in the three regular declensions. For we enjoy rich social lives and long to say (for example) 'to the soldier' and 'to the duke' or, as it may be, 'to the virgins' and 'to the slaves' (we move in very mixed company).

Rev up the brain-cells, then, and pay attention.

Datives galore

10b The datives we have met so far have included *mih-i, tib-i, e-i* (*s*) and *nob-is, vob-is, e-is* (*pl*). Aha, you swiftly conclude, *-i* must be a dat. *s* ending and *-is* a dat. *pl* ending. And so it turns out to be – in part.

1st decl. *puell-a*

> *puell-ae dixit*: he spoke to the girl.
> *puell-is dixit*: he spoke to the girls.

Exercise

Form the dat. *s* and *pl* of *serva, puella, luna, stella*.
Translate: *quid lunae dicis, lunatice?; noli servis respondere;*

77

puellis vinum dat; Iesus dixit servae; homo nihil (nothing) *servis respondit; mater non servis sed puellis prandium dedit* (*ded-i* is the perfect of *do*); *Angle, da mihi et servae aquam.*

10c 2nd decl. *serv-us*

serv-o dixit: he spoke to the slave.
serv-is dixit: he spoke to the slaves.

Exercise

Form the dat *s* and *pl* of: *angelus, deus, mundus, Normannus, Anglus.*

Translate: *angelo dic, Angle; Deus filium* (son) *mundo dedit; servi, date Normannis prandium; milites duci dixerunt; quid Normanno respondisti?; non servo sed militibus aquam dederunt.*

10d 3rd decl. *dux (duc-)*

duc-i dixit: he spoke to the duke.
duc-ibus dixit: he spoke to the dukes.

Exercise

Form the dat. *s* and *pl* of: *pater, mater, mulier, navis, virgo, miles* (n.b. you must find out the stem of these words before you can attach the dat. ending to them: see **6c**).

Translate: *cur patri dixerunt?; nunc miles regi respondet; milites semper ducibus responderunt; nolite, patres, militibus dicere; homo virgini aquam dare non potuit; quid mulieri dedisti, rex?*

eo 'I go'

10e The only seriously potty verb we have met so far is the verb 'to be' (*sum esse fui*) – as potty in English ('I *am*, to *be*, I *was*') as in Latin. Here is another slightly potty, and very common, verb: *eo* 'I go'. Its principal parts are *eo ire* ('to go') *iv-i* or *i-i* 'I went' (you see? 'Go – went': potty in English too).

As you can see, its basic stem is *i-*. It conjugates in the present: *e-o* ('I go'), *i-s* ('you go', etc), *i-t, i-mus, i-tis, e-unt.*

Qvid lvnae dicis
lvnatice?

Its imperative forms (go!) are *i!* (*s*), *i-te!* (*pl*).

Its perfect stem is *iv-* or *i-*, and it adds the regular perfect endings: thus 'I went' *i(v)-i, i(v)-isti, i(v)-it, i(v)-imus, i(v)-istis, i(v)-erunt*.

Exercise

Translate into Latin: I go, you (*pl*) went, they go, he went, go! (*pl*), they went, he goes, we went, you (*s*) go, do not (*s*) go!, they cannot go.

Turn coming into going (e.g. *venis* 'you come' = *is* 'you go': get the right tense!): *venistis, venitis, venerunt, veniunt*.

Turn going into coming: *ivit, ite!, imus, iverunt, ivistis, itis, eunt, iisti*.

St Jerome

10f RECORD the vocabulary: *qui* (he/you/they) who; *anim-a* life n. 1f; *suam* his (goes with 'life'); *od-i* I hate (note: perfect in form – *odi odisti odit* etc. – but present in meaning); *custodi-o* 4v guard; *diligo* 3v *dilexi* love; *inimic-us* enemy n. 2m; *si* if; *quae gratia* what thanks?.

Translate: St John 12.25 *qui amat animam suam, perdet* (will lose) *eam; et qui odit animam suam in hoc* (this) *mundo, in vitam aeternam custodit eam;* St Luke 6.27 *sed vobis dico qui auditis: diligite inimicos vestros* (your), *benefacite* (do good) *his* (to them) *qui oderunt ... si diligitis eos qui vos diligunt, quae vobis est gratia? ... diligite inimicos vestros, benefacite et mutuum* (loan) *date*.

Answers

10b *servae, servis; puellae, puellis; lunae, lunis; stellae, stellis.* what are you saying to the moon, lunatic?; do not reply to the slaves; he gives wine to the girls; Jesus said to the slave; the fellow replied nothing to the slaves; mother gave dinner not to the slaves but to the girls; Englishman, give me and the slave water.

10c *angelo, angelis; deo, deis; mundo, mundis; Normanno Normannis; Anglo Anglis.*
Speak to the angel, Englishman; God gave his son to the world; slaves, give (to) the Normans dinner; the soldiers spoke to the duke; what did you reply to the Norman?; they gave water not to the slave but to the soldiers.

10d *patri, patribus; matri, matribus; mulieri, mulieribus; navi, navibus; virgini, virginibus; militi, militibus.*
Why did they say to father?; now the soldier replies to the king; the soldiers always replied to the leaders; fathers, do not talk to the soldiers; the fellow could not give water to the young girl; what did you give to the woman, king?

10e *eo, i(v)istis, eunt, i(v)it, ite, i(v)erunt, it, i(v)imus, is, noli ire!; ire non possunt.*
i(v)istis, itis, i(v)erunt, eunt.
venit, venite!, venimus, venerunt, venistis, venitis, veniunt, venisti.

10f Who loves his life will lose it, and who hates his life in this world guards it into life eternal; but I say to you who listen, love your enemies, do good to them who hate (you) ... if you love those who love you, what thanks is there for you? ... love your enemies, do good and give (them) a loan.

The world of Rome

An emperor's legacy

One of the most interesting documents to come down to us from the ancient world is the 'Record of achievements and expenditure' which the first Roman emperor Augustus (31 BC – AD 14) had fixed to the front of his mausoleum in Rome (*res gestae*, 'things done', as it is called in its abbreviated form). It is known to us from a copy in Latin and Greek found in Turkey. It is not a complete record of Augustus' reign, omitting as it does anything unfavourable to him, but contains fascinating information.

Augustus tells, for example, of holding three censuses, when the number of Roman citizens rose from just over four million to nearly five million; he spent over 2,400 million sesterces (a *sestertius* = roughly £1) to reward soldiers, buy land for them and appease the plebs; he restored eighty-two temples, and the main road from Rome to Rimini; and put on 26 shows at which 3,500 African beasts were destroyed, and a naval battle in which 3,000 men took part. He lists the huge number of honours and titles the Romans gave him, and ends by suggesting the most important title of all was *Pater Patriae* – 'Father of the Country'.

He would, wouldn't he? The Roman historian Tacitus puts a different gloss on it. Augustus was buying Romans' liberty. His reign was a *dominatio*.

Word play

Augustus is a very interesting name. It is derived from *augeo*, 'increase, enlarge', which has another stem *auct-*. Hence auction and author, originally *auctor*, an increaser, or founder (and so also an authority). An augment is an increase, and *aug-silium* (*auxilium*) an increase especially in forces – hence auxiliary, or help. An augur is probably one who predicts increase, i.e. success, and the name Augustus means 'consecrated by the augurs' or 'undertaken under favourable auspices' (he gave his name to the month of August). The following places all take their name from Augustus: Autun (Augustodunum), Val d'Aosta (Augusta), and Zaragoza (Caesar-augusta).

CHAPTER 11

The imperfect enjoyment

You are at the half-way work. You have been working too hard. You need a rest. So in this chapter we introduce only one very simple new thing – enough to drive you bats – and devote the rest to some of the joys of a Latin Christmas.

The imperfect

11a Here is a completely new tense.

Say after me: *-bam, -bas, -bat, -bamus, -batis, -bant.*
That's it. Good, regular language, Latin.

These are the endings of the imperfect tense, meaning 'I was doing/used to do X'. It indicates the action continued or was habitual over a period of time in the past. So *amabam*, I was loving, I used to love, *monebam*, I was warning, I used to warn, and so on (see **Word play** in **Chapter 8**).

In other words, it's a case of (yawn) present stem + key vowel + endings, viz:

1s	*am-a-ba-m*	'I was loving, used to love'
2s	*am-a-ba-s*	'you were loving, used to love'
3s	*am-a-ba-t*	'he/she/it was loving, used to love'
1pl	*am-a-ba-mus*	'we were loving, used to love'
2pl	*am-a-ba-tis*	'you were loving, used to love
3pl	*am-a-ba-nt*	'they were loving, used to love'

So: 2nd conj. *mon-e-bam*; 3rd conj. *reg-e-bam*; 4th conj. *aud-ie-bam*; 5th conj. *cap-ie-bam*.

Remember: the imperfect drives you *-bam -bas -bat*-s. Remember also to keep a grip on your stems. The imperfect is based on the present stem (with imperfect endings). Compare the perfect – based on the perfect stem (the 3rd p.p.) with perfect endings.

Exercise

Translate: *amabamus, habebant, iubebas, ducebatis, regebant, faciebat, dicebant, trahebatis, capiebam, creabant, interrogabas.*

He was believing, she was delighting, they were knowing, he was not knowing, you (*s*) were listening, they were carrying, he was warning, you (*pl*) were ordering.

11b *sum* 'I am' is, as usual, as mad as a hatter. In the imperfect ('I was', 'you were', etc) it conjugates:

era-m, era-s, era-t, era-mus, era-tis, era-nt.

And what do you think the imperfect of *possum* 'I am able/can' is? Correct – *pot + eram*:

pot-eram 'I was able/could', *pot-eras, pot-erat, pot-eramus, pot-eratis, pot-erant.*

Note also the imperfect of *eo* 'I go': *i-bam* 'I was going', *i-bas, i-bat, i-bamus, i-batis, i-bant.*

Exercise

Turn these present forms into the equivalent imperfect forms: *sum, possumus, itis, potes, sunt, eo, est, it.*

Turn these imperfect forms into the equivalent perfect (tricky! You will need the perfect stem. See **8d** and **10e** for relevant perfect stems):

eratis, erant, poterat, ibam, poteratis, ibas, poterant, erat.

Translate (taking the 'was' form as imperfect): I was, she has been, we were able, they were going, they have been, she was, you (*pl*) were going.

Exercise

Translate: *duces et reges in silvam ibant cum servis; quid mihi et ei dicebas? milites ad naves ire non poterant; puella nobis et vobis prandium dabat; cur, homo, aquam virgini dare non poteras? ibat dux et portabat militibus arma* (weapons, acc.).

amabamus iubebas faciebat

dicebant trahebatis interrogabas

St John 1.1-5

11c Vocabulary: *apud* + acc. with; *hoc* this; *omnia* all things; *per* + acc. through; *facta sunt* were made; *factum est* was made; *sine* + abl. without; *ips-* him; *nihil* nothing; *quod* which; *lux* light; *hominum* of men; *luceo* shine; *comprehendo* overwhelm.

in principio erat verbum et verbum erat apud Deum, et Deus erat verbum. hoc erat in principio apud Deum. omnia per ipsum facta sunt: et sine ipso factum est nihil quod factum est. in ipso vita erat, et vita erat lux hominum. et lux in tenebris lucet, et tenebrae eam non comprehenderunt.

85

adeste, fideles

11d Vocabulary: *adeste* be present (imperative of *adsum*); *fidelis* faithful (one); *laetus* happy; *triumphans* (*triumphant-*) triumphant; *nat-us* child 2m; *angelorum* of angels; *adoremus* (subjunctive) let us adore; *Domin-us* Lord 2m.

> *adeste, fideles,*
> *laeti triumphantes*
> *venite, venite in Bethleem.*
> *natum videte,*
> *regem angelorum!*
> *venite, adoremus*
> *Dominum.*

Note: before he became Pope (Gregory the Great, 590-604 AD), Gregory saw some young, blond, handsome English boys for sale in Rome. Asked who they were, he was told they were called *Angli*. He replied *'bene, nam et angelicam habent faciem'* – 'Good, for they have *angelic* faces too'. He immediately asked the Pope to send missionaries to convert these *Ang(e)li*.

St Luke 2: the birth of Christ

11e Vocabulary: *ill-* he/(*pl*) they; *ecce* behold; *enim* for (first word); *evangelizo* announce; *gaudium* joy; *magnum* great; *quod erit* which shall be; *omnis* all; *populus* people; *quia* because; *natus est* there is born; *hodie* today; *Salvator* saviour; *qui* who; *dominus* lord; *civitas* (*civitat-*) city; *hoc* this; *signum* sign; *invenietis* you will find; *infans* (*infant-*) child; *pannis* in swaddling clothes; *involutus* wrapped; *positus* placed; *praesepium* manger.

et dixit illis angelus 'nolite timere: ecce enim evangelizo vobis gaudium magnum quod erit omni populo: quia natus est vobis hodie salvator, qui est Christus Dominus, in civitate David, et hoc vobis signum: invenietis infantem pannis involutum, et positum in praesepio'.

Answers

11a We were loving, they were having, you (*s*) were ordering, you (*pl*) were leading, they were ruling, he was making, they were saying, you (*pl*) were dragging, I was capturing, they were creating, you (*s*) were asking.
credebat, delectabat, sciebant, nesciebat, audiebas, portabant, monebat, iubebatis.

11b *eram, poteramus, ibatis, poteras, erant, ibam, erat, ibat.*
fuistis, fuerunt, potuit, i(v)i, potuistis, i(v)isti, potuerunt, fuit.
eram, fuit, poteramus, ibant, fuerunt, erat, ibatis.
Generals and kings were going into the wood with slaves; what were you saying to me and him?; the soldiers were unable to go to the ships; the girl was giving us and you dinner; why, fellow, were you unable to give water to the girl?; the general was going and carrying weapons for the soldiers.

11c In the beginning was the word, and the word was with God and the word was God. This was in the beginning with God. All things were made by him: and without him was made nothing which was made. In him was life, and the life was the light of men. And the light shines in the shadows, and the shadows did not overwhelm it.

11d Come, faithful (ones), happy, triumphant, come, come into Bethlehem. See the child, king of angels! Come, let us adore the Lord.

11e And the angel said to them 'Do not be afraid: for behold, I announce to you great joy which shall be to all people: because for you is born today a Saviour, who is Christ the Lord, in the city (of) David, and this for you (shall be) the sign: you will find the infant wrapped in swaddling clothes, and placed in a manger'.

The world of Rome

Worshipping strange gods

Romans in general were liberal about worship of the gods. After all, a foreign god might turn out to be more powerful than your own. It was prudent, therefore, to welcome them all in. So Egyptian gods like Isis and Serapis had their cult following in

Rome, and Romans invited in the cult of Cybele from Asia Minor to help in the war against Hannibal.

Why, then, did they take against Christianity? The point was that the Roman authorities liked to be in control of their cults. State and religion were inextricably entwined (all major priests were senators, and omens were taken before meetings). Cults were permitted only on condition that they became part of that nexus. Any religion that seemed to pose a threat to Roman order was stamped on. So in 186 BC, when the Bacchanalia, the religious rites of Dionysus, got out of hand, leading to crime and social unrest, the cult was banned.

Christianity, with its refusal (like Judaism) to countenance any other but the one true, God and in particular its promise of a new world order, clearly broke the rules. In the next chapter we look at a famous correspondence on the matter between the younger Pliny (governor of northern-eastern Turkey *c.* AD 110-112) and his emperor Trajan.

Word play

QED stands for *quod erat demonstrandum* – 'that which/what was to-be-proved' at the start of the theorem, and now has been. *demonstro* 1v means 'show, prove', and the *-ndum* form is known as the gerundive. It means 'requiring/needing/to be -ed'. Amanda means 'needing to be loved' (note the feminine *-a* ending, like *puell-a*). *propaganda* are 'things that need to be propagated' (*propago* 1v), and the *-a* ending in this case is neuter plural (like *bell-a*). *agenda* are 'things that need to be acted on' (*ago* 3v, 'do, act on') – one thing that needs to be acted on should be an *agendum*. *desideranda* are 'things that are to be desired', unlike *desiderata* which are 'things that have been desired' (see **14g**). *delenda est Carthago* means 'Carthage is to be destroyed' (see **World of Rome** in **Chapter 8**).

CHAPTER 12

Perfect fulfilment

12a After the last chapter's '*bat*-ty' imperfect enjoyment ('I was -ing'), back to the perfects, like *rex-i* 'I (have) ruled, did rule'. We first met them a thousand years ago in **Chapter Eight**. They were formed out of the 3rd principal part, + endings *-i, -isti, -it, -imus, -istis, -erunt*. We were disheartened to learn there that the 3rd p.p.s of 3rd and 5th conj. verbs were all irregular, but good news was promised on the subject of 3rd p.p.s of the other conjugations.

Here it is. The 3rd p.p.s of 1st, 2nd and 4th conjugation verbs are divinely regular, restoring our faith in the language (if we ever lost it). All you have to remember is *-vi* and *-ui*.

RECORD them all.

1st conjugation

12b *am-o 1v am-are* **ama-v-i** '**I have loved/loved/did love**'. All 1st conj. verbs form their perfects like this: stem + key vowel *-a-* + *v-i, v-isti, v-it* etc. (as at 8b-c). Thus *equit-o 1v equit-are* **equita-v-i** '**I rode**', *pugn-o 1v pugn-are* **pugna-v-i** '**I fought**', *port-o 1v port-are* **porta-v-i** '**I carried**', and so on.

RECORD two common exceptions: *d-o 1v d-are* **ded-i** '**I gave**' and *st-o 1v st-are* **stet-i** '**I stood**'.

Exercise

Translate: *dedisti, portaverunt, festinavit, portabas, nuntiavi, ministraverunt, dabat, stetimus, stabat mater dolorosa* (lamenting), *amavistis, pugnavi, pugnabamus*.

I stood, we fought, they rode, she carried, they gave, he loved.

dedisti | portaverunt

festinavit | portabas

2nd conjugation

12c *mone-o 2v mone-re **mon-u-i** 'I warned'*, i.e. stem + *u-i*, *u-isti, u-it* etc. Slightly odd, this dropping of the *-e-* and replacement with *-u-*, but there it is – that is the regular formation.

Thus e.g, *habe-o 2v habe-re **hab-u-i** 'I had'*, *tene-o 2v tene-re* **ten-u-i** 'I held'.

Remember: you have already met the irregular *vide-o 2v vide-re* **vid-i** 'I saw', *iube-o 2v iube-re* **iuss-i** 'I ordered' and *responde-o 2v responde-re* **respond-i** 'I replied'.

Exercise

Translate: *monuit, iussimus, habuimus, iubebant, tenuerunt, respondit, monebatis, viderunt, habui, monuimus, monebamus, monemus.*

They warned, you (*s*) ordered, he had, they terrified (*terreo terrere terr-u-i*), we replied, we are replying, he held, I saw.

4th conjugation

12d *audi-o 4v audi-re **aud-i-v-i** '*I heard'*. Note stem + key vowel *-i-* + *v-i, v-isti v-it*, etc.

Please stop yawning at the back there. Yes, I know it's boring but that's what comes of Latin being such a good, regular language. You should be *pleased* it is so boring.

Thus e.g. *sci-o 4v sci-re **sc-i-vi** 'I knew'*, *nesci-o 4v nescire **nesc-i-vi** 'I did not know'*, etc.

Note you have already met the irregular *senti-o 4v senti-re **sens-i** 'I felt'* and *veni-o 4v veni-re **ven-i** 'I came'*.

Exercise

Translate: *audivisti, nescivit, sciverunt, venit, sensi, nescivistis, sciebam, audiverunt, nescivi, sentiebat.*

You (*s*) knew, we did not know, they felt, he guarded (*custodio custodire custodivi*), they came, she heard.

Participles

12e Examine:
   Iesus respondit, dicens: Jesus replied, saying.
   discipuli responderunt, dicentes: the disciples replied, saying.
   homo venit, vinum portans: the man came, carrying wine.
   viderunt hominem venientem et vinum portantem: they saw the fellow coming and carrying wine.

A participle is a verb ending in '-ing' in English (not quite true, but it will do for the moment).

In Latin, it ends in *-ns* in the nom. *s* and *-ntem* in the acc. *s*, and *-ntes* in the nom. and acc. *pl*, and that is how we shall use it for the moment.

12f Stifling a yawn, guess how you form the participle of the five conjugations. That's right (stifle): present stem + key vowel + *-ns* (nom. *s*) or *-ntes* (nom. *pl*).

Thus: *amans, amantes* 'loving': *monens monentes* 'warning': *regens regentes* 'ruling': *audiens audientes* 'hearing': *capiens capientes* 'capturing'.

Observe that *amans*, as well as meaning 'loving', can also mean 'a person loving/a person who loves/ a lover'. So the poet Ovid says *militat omnis* (=every) *amans* – 'Every lover plays the soldier'.

Exercise

Translate: *omnis* (everyone, nom.) *amantem amat; Iesus respondens ei dixit; milites, clamantes* (*clamo* 1v 'shout') *et festinantes, ad palatium ibant; vidi hominem ex aqua equitantem; servum interrogantes, milites nullam causam in eo inveniebant* (see **12g** vocabulary).

St John 19.4-6

12g Note the vocabulary: *ergo* so; *iterum* again; *foras* outside; *ecce* behold; *adduco* lead/bring out; *invenio* (4) find; *nullam ... causam* no fault; *clamo* (1) shout; *crucifigo* (3) crucify; *accipio* (5) take, receive; *enim* (translate as first word) for.

exivit ergo iterum Pilatus foras, et dicit eis: ecce adduco eum (= Jesus) *vobis foras, ut* (that) *cognoscatis* (you may know) *quia* (that) *nullam invenio in eo causam. exivit ergo Iesus portans coronam* (crown) *spineam* (of thorns) *et purpureum vestimentum. et (Pilatus) dicit eis: ecce homo. clamabant dicentes, crucifige, crucifige eum. dicit eis Pilatus: accipite eum vos, et crucifigite; ego enim non invenio in eo causam.*

Answers

12b You gave, they carried, he hurried, you were carrying, I announced, they served, he was giving, we stood, mother was standing lamenting, you loved, I fought, we were fighting.

steti, pugnavimus, equitaverunt, portavit, dederunt, amavit.

12c He warned, we ordered, we had, they were ordering, they took, he replied, you were warning, they saw, I had, we warned, we were warning, we warn.

monuerunt, iussisti, habuit, terruerunt, respondimus, respondemus, tenuit, vidi.

12d You heard, he did not know, they knew, he came, I felt, you did not know, I was knowing, they heard, I did not know, he was feeling.

scivisti, nescivimus, senserunt, custodivit, venerunt, audivit.

12f Everyone loves a lover; Jesus replying said to him; the soldiers, shouting and hurrying, were going to the palace; I saw the fellow riding out of the water; questioning the slave, the soldiers found no fault in him.

12g So Pilate therefore came out again and says to them: behold, I bring him outside to you, so that you may know that I find no fault in him. Jesus therefore came out wearing a crown of thorns and a purple robe and (Pilate) says to them: behold, the fellow. They shouted, saying Crucify, crucify him. Pilate says to them: you take him and crucify (him): for I do not find fault in him.

The world of Rome

Dealing with Christians

As we saw last week, Romans were liberal about worship, except where a sect posed a threat to Roman order. Christianity, with its promise of a new world order, was one such sect. We possess a letter from Pliny the Younger, governor of Bithynia (northeast Turkey) AD 110-112, to the emperor Trajan seeking approval for his method of dealing with the problem.

Pliny's test, he tells us, was 'to invite the accused to deny that they had ever been Christians; then to repeat after me a formula of invocation to pagan gods; and then make offerings of wine and incense to Trajan's statue (which I had brought into the court, along with images of the gods), and revile the name of Christ – none of which, I understand, any genuine Christian can be induced to do'.

Trajan commends Pliny's approach, agreeing that general rules and formulas in such cases are impossible. He says there must be no witch hunts; those who repent of their Christianity are to be released; and Pliny must pay no attention to 'anonymously circulated pamphlets' naming Christians, which 'create the worst sort of precedent and are out of keeping with the spirit of the age'.

Word play

As we have seen, participles have a stem in *-ant-* or *-ent-*. These yield a huge range of words in English (provident, mutant, militant, deterrent, consonant, and so on) but bring a nice little problem along with them – should these words end in *-ant* or *-ent*? If it was a matter to be decided purely on Latin grounds, there would be no problem: first conj. verbs would end in *-ant*, all the rest in *-ent* (or *-ient*, e.g. gradient).

But consider dependent – or should that be dependant? The Latin verb is *dependo*, third conjugation. Surely, therefore, dependent? Yes indeed, if dependent is an adjective, e.g. he is dependent on me; we are all dependent on the state; and so on. But when it is a noun, dependant is correct, e.g. he is a dependant of his parents. The reason for this is that the noun is primarily a legal term, and came into English via French. All French participles end in *-ant*; the French participle *dependant* was picked up in English as a noun; so dependant is the correct spelling for the noun in English.

CHAPTER 13

We turn into reporters of Catullus' love

volo, nolo, malo

13a We already have two very useful specimens in our museum of potty verbs – *sum* 'I am' and *eo* 'I go'. Here are three more corkers for the display case, all of them related.

The principal parts of *vol-o* 'I wish, want' are *vol-o velle volu-i*. It conjugates in the present:

1*s*	*volo*	'I wish'
2*s*	*vis*	
3*s*	*vult*	
1*pl*	*volumus*	
2*pl*	*vultis*	
3*pl*	*volunt*	

Two other verbs are based on it:

(i) *nolo nolle nolu-i* 'I do not want, refuse' combines *non* + *volo* and conjugates

1*s*	*nolo*	'I refuse'
2*s*	*non vis*	
3*s*	*non vult*	
1*pl*	*nolumus*	
2*pl*	*non vultis*	
3*pl*	*nolunt*	

We have already met its imperative form *noli / nolite* (**5e**).

(ii) *malo malle malu-i* 'I prefer' combines *magis* 'more' with *volo* and conjugates:

95

1s   *malo*   'I prefer'
2s   *mavis*
3s   *mavult*
1pl   *malumus*
2pl   *mavultis*
3pl   *malunt*

Note: these verbs are followed by an infinitive, as in English. Thus: I prefer to go: *malo ire*.

Exercise

Translate: *festinare non vult, cur vis ire?, venire malumus, venire maluimus, nolle, videre volunt, malle, vultis, equitare noluit, nescire mavis, ire volebamus, audire nolumus, audire noluimus, dicere mavultis, facere voluerunt.*

    They wish to go, you (*pl*) prefer to come, he refuses to hear, to prefer, he wishes to ride, we did not want to make, to wish, they preferred to lead, to refuse.

The acc. and inf.

13b Scrutinise and translate: *dico Willelmum esse ducem.* Word for word – 'I say William to be duke'. Put it into English: 'I say *that* William *is* duke'.

    Now try: *scio Haroldum regere Anglos.* Word for word – 'I know Harold to rule/to be ruling the English', i.e. I know *that* Harold *rules* the English.

    And again: *nuntiavit Caesarem ducere milites* – 'he announced Caesar to lead/to be leading the soldiers', i.e. 'he announced *that* Caesar *was leading* the soldiers'.

13c We are dealing here with what is called 'reported' or 'indirect' speech. The give-away in English is verbs of saying, thinking, knowing, reporting, feeling (etc. – what comes from the mouth, brain or heart, in other words) THAT something is the case. In Latin, there is no give-away 'that'. The subject of the 'that' clause goes into the acc., the verb into the infinitive.

    The way to handle the Latin is to translate the Latin literally first of all, awkward though it is, and then convert it to the English 'that' form.

13d One little wrinkle that sometimes emerges is that, since the subject of an indirect statement is in the acc., the place seems to be crawling with accs. The question then becomes – which is the subject? For example, *scio Haroldum Anglos regere* could mean either 'I know that Harold rules the English' or 'that the English rule Harold'. In general, take the first acc. as subject.

13e Note *se*, 'him/her/them' (cf. French *se*) refers to the person speaking/thinking. Thus *Caesar dicit se ducem esse* means 'Caesar says him (Caesar) to be leader'. *Caesar dicit eum ducem esse* means 'Caesar says him (someone else) to be leader'.

Note also *Caesar negat eum ducem esse* 'Caesar denies that he is leader' or 'says that he is not leader'. Latin does not use *dico ... non* for this purpose.

Vocabulary

Note: *ali-us quam* anyone other than; *amica* female friend, whore 1f; *bene volo* wish well (to/for + dat.); *cogo* 3 *cogere coegi* compel; *desisto* 3 *desistere destiti* leave off, desist (from, + infin., i.e. he desists from going = *desistit ire*); *diligo* 3 *diligere dilexi* love; *iniuri-a* hurt, injury (of Catullus' broken love) 1f; *gnat-us* child 2m; *magis* more; *minus* less; *nec ... nec* neither ... nor; *nego* 1 deny, say that ... not; *nubo* 3 *nubere nupsi* marry (+ dat., i.e. she marries me = *mihi nubit*); *nulli* (dat.) no one; *od-i* (conjugated as a perfect – *odi odisti odit* etc. – but present in meaning) I hate; *quare* = *cur*, why?; *se* him/her/them (talking about the subject); *si* if; *tantum ... quantum* so much ... as; *vulgus* mob 2n.

Exercise

Lesbia was the mistress of the Roman poet Catullus. They enjoyed a stormy relationship, which Catullus reported at length in his poetry, from which most of the following sentences are adapted.

Translate: *scio Catullum Lesbiam amare; Lesbia dixit se*

Scio Catullum Lesbiam amare | Lesbia dixit se amare Catullum

Catullus dixit eum amare Lesbiam | Lesbia negavit se amare alium quam Catullum

amare Catullum; Catullus dixit eum amare Lesbiam; Catullus negat Lesbiam se amare; Lesbia negavit se amare alium quam Catullum; Catullus Lesbiam amare non desistebat; Catullus Lesbiam nec amabat nec bene volebat; quare Catullus Lesbiam odit et amat? nescit Catullus, sed sentit; Lesbia, quare negavisti te alium quam Catullum amare posse? Catullus negabat se Lesbiae bene velle; Lesbia nulli quam Catullo nubere vult; Lesbia dixit se nulli quam Catullo nubere malle; iniuria Catullum cogit Lesbiam amare magis, sed bene velle minus; Catullus Lesbiam dilexit non tantum ut (=as) vulgus [diligit] amicam, sed ut pater [diligit] gnatos; quare Lesbiae non bene vis, Catulle? Lesbia *dicebat se velle Catullo nubere; Lesbia negavit eam Catullo nubere velle.*

Answers

13a He refuses to hurry, why do you want to go?, we prefer to come, we preferred to come, to refuse, they wish to see, to prefer, you want, he refused to ride, you prefer not to know, we were wishing to go, we refuse to hear, we refused to hear, you prefer to speak, they wished to do.
ire volunt, venire mavultis, audire non vult, malle, equitare vult, facere noluimus, velle, ducere maluerunt, nolle.

13e I know that Catullus loves Lesbia; Lesbia said that she loved Catullus; Catullus said that he (= someone else) loved Lesbia; Catullus says that he (?Lesbia) does not love Lesbia (?him); Lesbia said that she did not love anyone other than Catullus; Catullus did not stop loving Lesbia; Catullus did not love Lesbia nor wish her well; why does Catullus hate and love Lesbia? Catullus does not know, but he feels (it); Lesbia, why did you deny that you could love anyone other than Catullus?; Catullus was denying that he wished Lesbia well; Lesbia wishes to marry no one (other) than Catullus; Lesbia said that she preferred to marry no one (other) than Catullus; the pain compels Catullus to love Lesbia more, but wish well (for her) less; Catullus loved Lesbia not so much as a mob [loves] its whore, but as a father [loves] his children; why do you not wish well for Lesbia, Catullus?; Lesbia was saying that she wanted to marry Catullus; Lesbia denied that she (= someone else) wanted to marry Catullus.

The world of Rome

Caesar in Britain

In 55 BC Julius Caesar crossed from Gaul (France) into Britain. He wanted both to create allies there who would dissuade British Celts from helping Gallic Celts revolt against Roman rule in Gaul, and to cause a splash at Rome. Britain was unknown, distant, romantic territory – Caesar hoped to reap popular acclaim by venturing into it.

In fact the expeditions of 55 and 54 BC did not achieve much. Back in Rome, Cicero was politely scathing on the subject ('no silver anywhere, and no booty except slaves, few of whom can be expected to have had any sort of musical or literary education'), though he agreed it made a good subject for epic poetry ('the places, the people, the scenery, the customs ...'). It was all in strong contrast with Caesar's conquest of Gaul, which made him and his followers vast fortunes, none of which reached the Roman treasury (though it still had to fund his legions!). We hear reports of a million Gauls being slaughtered, and a million more enslaved.

The emperor Claudius finally made Britain a province in AD 43, but it was never completely subdued or 'romanized'. Roman troops were always stationed here till they pulled out for ever in AD 410.

Word play

We looked at prefixes back in **Chapter 5**, but do not be misled by the little word *se* that we have just met. *se* as a pronoun means him(self), her(self), them(selves) – but it has nothing to do with the prefix *se-* .

se- as a prefix in Latin means 'apart, aside, without'. *securus* means 'without care' (*cura*); *seditio* is a going (*eo*) apart; *sedulus* means 'without tricks' (*dolus*, 'trick'); *secretus* means 'separated apart' (Latin *cerno*, stem *cret-* 'sift'), whence English 'secret' and 'secretary' (someone who deals with confidentialities); segregate means 'gather apart' (*grex* means 'herd'; cf. congregate, con- = *cum*, 'with'); seduce means 'lead aside'.

CHAPTER 14

Last principals

We get this chapter off to a flying start: two famous poems by the love poet Catullus. Both express his feelings about his mistress Lesbia. The word order in the second one is very tricky, but there is plenty of help at hand.

Love and hate

14a Vocabulary: *quare* why; *id* this (object of *faciam*); *faciam* I do (*faciam* is the subjunctive, gulp); *fortasse* perhaps; *requiro* 3 ask; *fieri* 'it-to-be-happening'; *excrucior* I am being tortured.

> *odi et amo. quare id faciam, fortasse requiris.*
> *nescio, sed fieri sentio et excrucior.*

Notice the contrast between doing and feeling. Catullus loves and hates. He is asked why he is *doing* it. It is not a matter of *doing*, he replies: he *feels* it *being* done to him and is tortured by it (literally 'crucified'). There is nothing he can *do* about it: it is beyond his control.

A woman's word

14b Vocabulary: *nulli ... quam* no one ... but; *se* her(self) (i.e. Lesbia, object of *dicit* and *petat*); *mea* my (with *mulier* = Lesbia); *Iuppiter ipse* Jupiter himself (subject); *petat* were to ask for (subjunctive again, tremble); *cupido ... amanti* to (her) ardent lover; *quod* what; *ventus* wind 2m; *rapida ... aqua* in racing water; *oportet* it is necessary; *scribo* 3 write.

nulli se dicit mulier mea nubere malle
quam mihi, non si se Iuppiter ipse petat.
dicit: sed mulier cupido quod dicit amanti,
in vento et rapida scribere oportet aqua.

Note: take line 1 in the order *mea mulier dicit se malle nubere nulli quam mihi.* Take line 3 *sed quod mulier dicit cupido amanti.* For metre, see pp. 143-4 below.

The 4th p.p.

14c So far we have met three 'principal parts' (p.p.), e.g. *amo* 1v *amare amavi.* You will now hardly be able to contain your excitement at learning that there is a final, 4th p.p. too, which completes the hand. Observe and **RECORD**:

    1st conj.:   *amo 1v amare amavi* **amat-um**
    2nd conj.:   *moneo 2v monere monui* **monit-um**
    4th conj.:   *audio 4v audire audivi* **audit-um**

14d Pretty gripping, you will agree. All regular 1st, 2nd and 4th conj. verbs form their 4th p.p. in this way: thus e.g. (1st) *portatum, ministratum, interrogatum, nuntiatum, datum*; (2nd) *habitum, territum*; (4th) *(ne)scitum, custoditum*.

14e But there is the usual collection of spanners in the ointment – or should that be flies in the works? – with our irregular verbs, especially in the 3rd and 5th conjugations. Among some of the most popular hits, please **RECORD** in particular:

    apprehendo 3v **apprehens-um**, *capio 5v* **capt-um**, *dico 3v* **dict-um**, *duco 3v* **duct-um**, *facio 5v* **fact-um**, *iubeo 2v* **iuss-um** *mitto 3v* **miss-um**, *rego 3v* **rect-um**, *respondeo 2v* **respons-um**, *sentio 4v* **sens-um**, *video 2v* **vis-um**, *vinco 3v* **vict-um**.

14f A linguistic note is worth intruding at this point. See how many English words we get from the 4th p.p. From *missum*, for example, we get mission, missive, missile, from *ductum* duct, product, ductile, induction, from *visum* vision, visible, and so on.

nulli se dicit mulier mea nubere
malle quam mihi, non si se Iuppiter
ipse petat

Meaning

14g Now, what does this 4th p.p. thingy actually *mean*? Briefly,
'having been -ed'. Thus *amatum* 'having been loved', *nuntiatum*
'having been announced', *portatum* 'having been carried', *rectum*
'having been ruled', *captum* 'having been captured', *visum* 'hav-

103

ing been see-ed:' (i.e. seen. Ha! Irregular in English too), *sensum* 'having been feel-ed' (i.e. felt) and so on.

14h But how is it used? The 4th p.p. is most commonly linked with *sum*, to form what is called the perfect passive. This takes the form 'I have been/was -ed'. Engage the brain in top gear and inspect the following:

1*s*   *amat-us* or *amat-a* or *amat-um* sum 'I have been *or* I was/loved'

2*s*   *amat-us a um es* 'you (*s*) have been *or* you were/loved'

3*s*   *amat-us a um est* 'he/she/it has been *or* he/she/it/was/loved'

1*pl* *amat-i ae a sumus* 'we have been *or* we were/loved'

2*pl* *amat-i ae a estis* 'you (*pl*) have been *or* you were/loved'

3*pl* *amat-i ae a sunt* 'they have been *or* they were/loved'

14i This may look rather nasty, but it is in fact as easy as pie.

amat-us shows that a man was loved. Thus *amatus est* means 'he was loved'.

amat-a means (wait for it) a woman was being loved. Thus *amata est* means 'she was loved'.

amat-um est means (yawn) something neuter was being loved. Thus *amatum est* means 'it was loved'.

Likewise in the plural: *amati* means men were loved, *amatae* women, and *amata* things.

You will at once see what is happening. *amat-* takes whatever ending is appropriate to describe the gender (m. f. or n.) of the person being loved. The m. endings tacked onto *amat-* are the same as m. nouns like *serv-us* 'male slave', the f. endings as f. nouns like *puell-a* 'girl' and n. endings as n. nouns like *bell-um* 'war'. Cinch, or what? (Cf. *Grammatical Summary*, 132)

Exercise

Translate, naming (where necessary) the gender of the person/thing -ed: *amatae estis, factum est, portati sunt, ducta est, custoditum est, captus es, visae sunt, victus sum, missi sumus,*

*iussa es, recti sunt, data sunt, nuntiatum est, interrogatae su-
mus.*

Turn these perfect actives into perfect passives. Remember
you will need to use the 4th p.p. and new endings. Thus e.g.
amaverunt 'they loved' will become *amat-i ae a sunt* 'they were
loved'.

amavit, duxerunt, misi, nuntiavimus, vidistis, vicerunt, cepit.

14j You will now be asking 'Oi, but why *amatus est*? *est* is
present – how can it mean something *was* done?' Good question.
A parallel can be drawn with e.g. English 'Dinner is served,
modom'. That does not mean dinner is *being* served (the true
present tense). It means it has been served: it's already done –
and is now there on the table awaiting the pleasure of the diners
gasping for the pail.

Answers

14a I hate and I love. Why I do this, perhaps you ask. I do not
know, but I feel it to be happening and I am tortured.
14b My woman says she prefers to marry no one but me, not
(even) if Jupiter himself were to ask for her. She speaks: but
what a woman says to her ardent lover, it is necessary to write
in the wind and racing water.
14i You (f.) were loved, it was done, they (m.) were carried, she
was led, it was guarded, you (m.) were captured, they (f.) were
seen, I (m.) was conquered, we (m.) were sent, you (f.) were
ordered, they (m.) were ruled, they (n.) were given, it was
announced, we (f.) were questioned.
*amat-us a um est, duct-i ae a sunt, miss-us a um sum, nuntiat-i
ae a sumus, vis-i ae a estis, vict-i ae a sunt, capt-us a um est.*

The world of Rome

Roman democracy

The Romans did not invent democracy (it was invented by the
Athenian Cleisthenes in 508 BC) but their version of it has been
very influential. Roman republican democracy, like ours, was
representative. The citizen body was divided up into assemblies
to appoint officials to the Senate and ratify laws. So, like us –

but quite unlike Greeks – citizens took no policy decisions themselves: they voted for officials to make decisions for them, though (unlike us) they then also voted to ratify those decisions that were to become law.

There were in fact three assemblies, and the people were divided into 'colleges' for voting purposes (one vote per 'college'). One assembly, for example, appointed consuls and praetors and declared war (voting here was weighted in favour of the landed rich). Features of this system were picked up by the inventors of American democracy in 1787, but perhaps the Romans' most important political contribution over the millennia has been its concept of world-wide citizenship. Anyone, of any race, could become a citizen of Rome. Note 'Rome', not 'Italy'. The city of Rome was the centre of empire and power: *Italia* was subject to it. Interestingly, we know of no Latin poet who was a native of Rome.

Word play

Analyzing words is terrific fun but caution is needed. Take transparent, parent, and preparation: the first comes from *pareo* meaning 'I appear, am visible', the second from *pareo* 'I obey', and the third from *paro* 'I get ready'.

Again, the fact that we can identify the Latin meaning does not mean we can identify the current meaning. Precarious, for example, means hazardous, or dangerous, but it is in fact based on the Latin stem *prec-*, meaning prayer: it was a situation so hopeless you could only pray about it. To transgress means to sin, but its Latin meaning is simply to step (*gress-*) across (*trans*). Decimate today means slaughter indiscriminately, but it originates from Latin *decimus* 'tenth' and refers to the practice of executing every tenth man as a way of punishing mutinous soldiers.

We may not like the current meaning, of course, but there is not much we can do about it. Gross errors, however, where meaning is seriously at stake and words can be lost to the language, need correction. To militate (*miles, milit-* 'soldier') means to adopt an aggressive stance: it must not be confused with mitigate (*mitis*), meaning to soften, lessen. Refute means to engage in argument against (*refuto*): reject (*reicio* 'throw back') means something quite different. When a spokesman says 'I refute that statement', one longs to cry out 'Go on, then, you great booby, refute it'. What they usually mean is 'I reject it'. Any idiot can do *that*. 'Refute' sounds so much grander.

CHAPTER 15

Battling weekly, or weakly, as we are with our cases – it's worse than going on holiday – what on earth do we need another one for? Console yourself with the thought that we have already been meeting the next case regularly, although we have not yet submitted it to the white-heat of our analytical skills. Here it comes, then:

The ablative

15a We first met this case aeons ago back in **5c**, where it needed no explanation because it followed certain prepositions (*e(x)* 'out of', *cum* 'with' and *in* 'in'). It will continue to be used largely with prepositions, but it is now time to hit it firmly on the head, stuff it and mount it in our grammatical showcase.

Bring therefore the trained senses to bear on the following:

1st decl. f.	*s*	*a(b) puell-a*: by/from the girl
	pl	*a(b) puell-is*: by/from the girls
2nd decl. m.	*s*	*a(b) serv-o*: by/from the slave
	pl	*a(b) serv-is*: by/from the slaves
2nd decl. n.	*s*	*a(b) bell-o*: from the war
	pl	*a(b) bell-is*: from the wars
3rd decl.m./f.	*s*	*a(b) duc-e*: by/from the general
	pl	*a(b) duc-ibus*: by/from the generals

15b So: 1st and 2nd decl. *s* ablatives end in -*a*/*o*; *pl* end in -*is*; 3rd decl. *s* ablatives end in -*e*, *pl* in -*ibus*.

Observe also the meanings of *a(b)*: 'by' (a person) or 'away from' (cf. *e(x)* 'out of'). *a(b)* with the ablative meaning 'by' a person is especially common after passive verbs, e.g. *ab eo nuntiatum est* 'it was announced by him'.

15c Record also 'by me' *a me*, 'by you' (*s*) *a te*, 'by us' *a nobis*, 'by you' (*pl*) *a vobis*, 'by him' *ab eo*, 'by her' *ab ea*, 'by them' *ab eis*. Note also the useful little idioms *mecum* 'with me', *tecum* 'with you', *nobiscum* 'with us' and *vobiscum* 'with you' (*pl*).

Exercise

Using *a(b)* + abl., say 'by' the *s* and *pl* of the following people. With 3rd decl. nouns, remember to get the right stem onto which to put the abl. endings (revise **Chapter 6**):

Anglus, Normannus, puella, dux, miles, mulier, pater, virgo.

Translate: *tu a duce coactus es* (*cogo* compel) *in proelium ire, ego a muliere; cur Caesar mecum ire volebat?; respondens Normanno, Anglus dixit se nolle ex aqua venire; ab hominibus ad palatium cum servis ducta est; Caesar a Britannia ad Galliam* (Gaul) *ire maluit; a militibus ad Pilatum vobiscum missi sunt; ab eis nuntiatum est Caesarem venire; homini respondens, Pilatus dixit se malle Iesum dimittere* (release).

Adjectives

15d Last week we saw that if you wanted to say 'he was loved' you said *amatus est*, if 'she was loved' *amata est*. *amatus*, 'loved', changed in response to the gender of the person loved.

This is a very useful principle. All adjectives, or describing words (e.g. big, little, red, grey, etc.), change in response to the person described. So they all have m., f. and n. forms to help them do so. They also often appear next to the noun they describe, usually after it – very considerate of them.

2/1 declension adjectives

15e 2/1 decl. adjs. follow the patterns of 2nd and 1st decl. nouns, and take the dictionary form e.g. *magn-us magn-a magn-um* (shortened to *magn-us a um*) (see *Grammatical Survey*, 132).

The *-us* forms are used when the adj. is describing masculine nouns;

the *-a* forms when it describes feminine nouns;

the *-um* forms when it describes neuter nouns.

110

Thus: nom. *s miles bonus*, the good soldier, but *virgo bona*, the good girl. In the nom. *pl milites boni, virgines bonae*, and so on.

RECORD: 2/1 adjs: *bon-us a um* good; *formos-us a um* beautiful; *long-us a um* long, tall; *magn-us a um* great, big; *mal-us a um* wicked, evil; *me-us a um* my, mine; *miser miser-a um* unhappy; *mult-us a um* much (*pl* many); *noster nostr-a um* our(s); *parv-us a um* small (*pl* few); *tot-us a um* complete(ly), total(ly), all over; *tu-us a um* your(s) (when 'you' are one person); *vester vestr-a um* your (*s*) (when 'you' are more than one person).

Note: assume *noster* and *vester* are funny forms for what we would expect to be *nostrus* and *vestrus*; assume likewise that *miser* is a funny form for *miserus*.

3rd decl. adjectives

3rd decl. adjs follow the pattern of 3rd decl. nouns and so keep the same forms in describing both m. and f. nouns (we ignore n.). Thus, *puella fortis* 'the brave girl' and *miles fortis* 'the brave soldier'. They decline like *nav-is* (revise **6c** and see *Grammatical Summary*, 133).

RECORD: *fort-is* brave; *omn-is* all, every(one); *nobili-is* noble; *trist-is* sad.

Exercise

Translate: *pater tuus parvus erat; mater mea bona et nobilis fuit; omnes milites nostri, in Britannia habitantes* (*habito* live), *miseri et tristes erant; ego multos homines fortes in Gallia vidi, tu multas puellas formosas; scio ducem nostrum bonum et nobilem esse; Caesar vidit milites omnes ad palatium festinantes; cur non vidisti malam puellam tuam cum meo malo homine fugientem* (*fugio* run off)?; *o puella, ego sum totus tuus; o Angle, ego tota tua sum; ars* (art) *longa, vita brevis* (short).

Answers

15c *ab Anglo, ab Anglis; a Normano, a Normannis; a puella, a puellis; a duce, a ducibus; a milite, a militibus; a muliere, a mulieribus; a patre, a patribus; a virgine, a virginibus.*
You were compelled by the leader to go to battle, I by the woman;

Pater tuus parvus erat

why did Caesar wish to go with me?; reply to the Norman, the Englishman said that he did not wish to come out of the water; she was led by the men to the palace with the slaves; Caesar preferred to go from Britain to Gaul; they were sent by the soldiers to Pilate with you; it was announced by them that Caesar was coming; replying to the man, Pilate said that he preferred to release Jesus.

15e Your father was little; my mother has been good and noble; all our soldiers, living in Britain, were unhappy and sad; I saw many brave men in Gaul, you (saw) many lovely girls; I think our leader is good and noble; Caesar saw all the soldiers hurrying to the palace; why did you not see your wicked girl running off with my wicked man?; girl, I am all yours; Englishman, I am all yours; art (is) long, life short.

The world of Rome

Women's liberation?

Traditionally the Roman *paterfamilias* had the power of life and death over all his household (we hear of fathers executing their sons for stepping out of line in battle). Yet by the 1st century BC married woman had remarkable freedom.

In early days, it seems that marriage ceremonies designed to hand the woman completely over into her husband's power were normal. But it was still possible to be married by cohabitation, and by the late republic, the ceremonies were less favoured, and marriage had commonly become a matter of living together. In these circumstances, all a wife had to do to avoid her husband's legal control (and thus, for example, retain control over all her property) was to spend three days a year apart from him. Nor were formal legalities required to end such a marriage – the couple simply separated, the children automatically going to the father. But freedom for the woman meant freedom for the man: *uxor, vade foras* 'woman, go outside' was all he needed to say to divorce her. Serial marriage was very common: one Vistilia held the record with seven children by six different husbands.

Yet Romans still held to the ideal of lifelong commitment. There is no neat connection between law, custom and belief.

Word play

On its own, the ablative means 'by' or 'with', showing the means by which or manner in which something is done. It is a very fruitful source of family mottoes. Try the following, all in the ablative. The family is named in brackets afterwards.

Vocabulary: *vi-s* force; *ment-* mind, thought; *virtut-* courage, virtue; *voluntat-* will; *industri-* industry; *labor-* work; *sp-* hope; *consili-* counsel; *fid-* faith.

non vi sed mente (Lincolne); *non vi sed virtute* (Ramsbotham); *non vi sed voluntate* (Boucher); *industria et labore* (McGallock); *industria et spe* (Warden); *industria et virtute* (Bolton); *consilio et virtute* (Rose-Lewin); *fide et amore* (Conway, Gardner, Hart, Seymour); *fide et labore* (Allan); *fide et spe* (Borthwick).

CHAPTER 16

Inspecting our genitives

Our grammatical trolley already groans under the weight of a mountain of cases (nom., voc., acc., dat., and abl.), and with a final heave we now hurl the last one onto the top of the pile – the genitive. But let us limber up with a little Catullus first.

Catullus

16a Here Catullus compares Quintia with Lesbia. Note vocabulary: *candid-us a um* fair; *rect-us a um* upright; *illud* that (word); *nam* for; *null-us a um* no; *venustas* charm 3f; *tam* so; take *nulla* (l. 4) with *mica*; take *magno* with *corpore* (body); *mica* grain 1f; *salis* of salt, wit; *quae* who; *cum* first; *pulcherrim-us a um* most lovely. (For metre, see pp. 143-4 below.)

> *Quintia formosa est multis; mihi candida, longa,*
> > *recta est*: so these individual points I admit.
> *totum illud 'formosa' nego: nam nulla venustas,*
> > *nulla in tam magno est corpore mica salis.*
> *Lesbia formosa est, quae, cum pulcherrima tota est,*
> > and second, on her own robs all the others of all their
> > > charms.

Vocabulary

16b RECORD the following new words for future, extensive use:
   1st decl: *coron-a* n. 1f crown; *ecclesi-a* n. 1f church; *fortun-a* n. 1f luck, chance; *sapienti-a* n. 1f wisdom.
   2nd decl: *cib-us* n. 2m food; *sanct-us* n. 2m saint, holy (man).
   3rd decl: *mens ment-* n. 3f mind.

Quintia formosa est multis; mihi
candida, longa, recta est.

Lesbia formosa est, quae, cum
pulcherrima tota est

3rd decl. neuter: *corpus corpor-* n. 3n body; *cor cord-* n. 3n heart; *mare mar-* n. 3n sea.

Note: 3rd decl. neuter nouns have the same nom. and acc. forms. The nom. and acc. *pl* forms end in *-a*. See *Grammatical Summary*, 128.

4th decl: *exercit-us*, acc. *exercit-um*, gen. *exercit-us* army.

cad-o 3v *cecid-i* be killed; *colo* 3v *colu-i cult-um* inhabit; *coquo* 3v cook; *ex-eo ire* depart from; *fuga vert-o* 3v *vert-i* turn in flight; *incendo* 3v burn; *interficio* 5v *interfec-i interfect-um* kill; *not-o* 1v note, mark; *nunti-o* 1v announce, inform; *praeparo* 1v prepare; *resideo* 2v sit down; *trans-eo ire* cross; *vivo* 3v live; *volvo* 3v roll, turn.

Adjectives: 2/1 *niger nigr-a um* black; *pulcher pulchr-a um* beautiful.

Adjectives: 3 *absens absent-* absent.

Fixed forms: *autem* however, but; *dum* while; *ecce* see!, behold!; *iam* now, already; *modo* now; *olim* once upon a time.

Genitival attraction

16c The gen. basically means 'of'. You know it already, of course. Consider e.g.:

curriculum vit-ae 'record *of* life'

anno Domin-i 'in the year *of* (our) Lord';

e.g. = *exempl-i gratia* 'for the sake *of* an example';

credo in unum Deum, factorem cael-i et terr-ae 'I believe in one God, maker *of* heaven and (*of*) earth';

honor-is causa 'for reason *of* honour';

in nomine Patr-is et Fili-i et Spirit-us sanct-i 'in the name *of* the Father and *of* the Son and *of* the Holy Spirit', etc.

See the *Grammatical Summary*, 124-128, and aim the creaking brain at the examples below.

16d 1st decl. (f): *puell-a*

*dux **puell-ae***: leader of the girl, the girl's leader.

*dux **puell-arum***: leader of the girls, the girls' leader.

Exercise

Give the gen *s* and *pl* of: *ecclesia, corona, stella.*

117

Translate: *sapientia meae puellae, propter stellam nostrae fortunae, corona magna ecclesiae, propter tenebras terrae vestrae, stellarum fortuna, multarum terrarum aqua.*

16e 2nd decl. (m): *serv-us*
*dux **serv-i***: leader of the slave.
*dux **serv-orum***: leader of the slaves.

16f 2nd decl. (n): *bell-um*
*dux **bell-i***: leader of war
*dux **bell-orum***: leader of wars.

Exercise

Give the gen *s* and *pl* of: *cibus, sanctus, Deus, principium, prandium, caelum.*

Translate: *in vita Christi, principium magni belli, vita sanctorum, propter prandium sancti, ex aqua caelorum, propter sapientiam sanctorum.*

16g 3rd decl.: *miles milit-*
*dux **milit-is***: leader of the soldier.
*dux **milit-um***: leader of the soldiers.
*dux **eius*** leader of him/her.
*dux **eorum** (m)/**earum** (f) leader of them.

Note: 3rd decl. adjs. like *fort-is* and *omn-is* have gen. *pl* in *-ium*, e.g. *fortium, omnium.*

Exercise

Give the gen. *s* and *pl* of *pater, mater, virgo.*

Translate: *ante principium mundi; omnium ducum dux; omnium regum rex; in mente et corde omnium sanctorum; dicunt Haroldum regem Anglorum omnium esse; hic est fortis exercitus Willelmi ducis; servi corpus regis nobilis portabant; nuntiant Christum esse stellam mundi; exercitus magnus Willelmi ducis e navibus exivit; milites Haroldi regis mare magnum transibant; olim magnus dux exercitus (gen.) Willelmi ducis eram, iam servus regis Haroldi sum; olim homines multi palatium regis magni colebant, nunc autem in aqua habitant.*

Answers

16a For many, Quintia is beautiful; for me, she is fair, tall, upright: *haec ego sic singula confiteor.* (But) I deny that total (word, i.e. totality) 'beautiful': for there is no charm, no grain of wit in so great a body. (Now) Lesbia *is* beautiful, who first is most lovely all over, *tum omnibus una omnes surripuit veneres.*
16d *ecclesiae, ecclesiarum; coronae coronarum; stellae stellarum.*

Wisdom of my girl; because of the star of our chance; the great crown of the church; because of the shadows of your land; the luck of the stars; the water of many lands.
16f *cibi ciborum; sancti sanctorum; Dei deorum; principii principiorum; prandii prandiorum; caeli caelorum.*

In the life of Christ; the beginning of the great war; life of the saints; on account of the saint's dinner; out of the water of the heavens; on account of the saints' wisdom.
16g *patris patrum; matris matrum; virginis virginum.*

Before the beginning of the word; leader of all leaders; king of all kings; in the mind and heart of all the saints; they say that Harold is king of all the English; here is the brave army of Duke William; the slaves were carrying the body of the noble king; they announce that Christ is sun of the world; the great army of Duke William came out from the ships; the soldiers of Harold the king were crossing the great sea; once I was the great leader of the army of Duke William, now I am slave of Harold the king; once many men inhabited the palace of the great king, now however they live in the water.

The world of Rome

Citizenship

What did it mean to be a Roman citizen? In Acts 22, Paul is about to be flogged when he informs the centurion that he is a Roman citizen. The centurion informs the garrison commander Claudius Lysias, who tells Paul that his own citizenship cost him a lot of money. Paul replies 'It was mine by birth'.

Paul was a Greek-speaking Jew from Tarsus in Cilicia (S.E.

Turkey). He had never been near Rome. Since Cilicia had become part of the Roman empire a hundred years earlier, Paul's father was a Roman citizen. So Paul was one too. Claudius Lysias, however, the Roman commander, was probably Greek by birth and a slave too, in the service of the emperor Claudius in Rome. He had bought his freedom, as he was entitled to do if he could raise the money and his master agreed, and a freed slave took on his master's status.

Given so many competing claims upon their sense of who they were and to whom or what they owed allegiance, it is very hard to say exactly what Paul and Claudius Lysias made of their Roman citizenship. Perhaps not much more than what we make of calling ourselves 'westerners' – except when a Roman citizen found himself about to be flogged.

Word play

It is wonderful what games are played by an innocent little word like *pes* (*ped-*), n. 3m 'foot'.

It is obviously akin to the ancient Greek for foot, *pous pod-*, which gives us octopus (eight feet), podium, antipodes (having the feet opposite) and tripod (three feet) (**Word play** in **Chapter 17** explains why *pes* and *pous* are so alike). The Latin gives us pedal, pedestrian, and even pawn (*pedo*, a foot-soldier, via old French *pion*). *expedio* means 'I get my feet out of (a trap)', whence expedient meaning advantageous, and expedite, get things moving. *impedio* means the reverse – 'put your feet in (a trap)' (eventually producing, via French, impeach!). Piedmont is an area at the foot of mountains (*mons, mont-*). Most unlikely of all, a pedigree, the register of lineage or descent, comes from *pes* (foot), *de* (of) and *grus* (crane), middle French *pié de grue*, the three-line mark like a bird's foot showing family succession.

CHAPTER 17

Energetic, forward-looking and dynamic as we Latinists are, there comes a time when we wish to sit back, relax a little and let things happen to us. That time has now come. Today therefore we enjoy a wholly passive experience.

But you had better record some new vocabulary first. The reason for this is that we are now approaching the home straight, when we will do nothing but read the Bayeux tapestry, *Carmina Burana* and St John. In the last chapter, we listed vocabulary for the first two; here comes St John.

Vocabulary

17a RECORD:

discipul-us n. 2m disciple; *monument-um* n. 2n tomb; *respons-um* n. 2n reply.

crux cruc- n. 3f cross; *frater fratr-* n. 3m brother; *lex leg-* n. 3f law; *pontifex pontific-* n. 3m leader; *potestas potestat-* n. 3f power; *sermo sermon-* n. 3m conversation, words; *soror soror-* n. 3f sister.

caput capit- n. 3n head.

accipio 5v *accepi* take, receive; *clamo* 1v shout; *crucifigo* 3v *crucifix-i* crucify; *debet* he ought; *dimitto* 3v *dimis-i* release; *fleo* 2v cry; *impono* 3v *imposu-i* place X (acc.) on (dat.); *ploro* 1v weep; *pono* 3v *posu-i* place; *quaero* 3v seek; *scribo* 3v *scrips-i script-um* write; *sedeo* 2v sit; *tango* 3v touch; *trado* 3v *tradid-i* hand over, give up.

Fixed forms: *tunc* then; *ergo* therefore; *nisi* unless, except; *propterea* therefore; *quia* that; *si* if; *ubi* where.

The pluperfect: 'had'

17b Recall our old, perfect friends:

amav-i 'I loved/have loved' (the perfect active).

amatus sum 'I was/have been loved' (the perfect passive).

Now peer beadily at these new, pluperfect ('more than perfect') friends:

Pluperfect active

1*s* *am-a-v-eram*	'I had loved'
2*s* *am-a-v-eras*	'you had loved'
3*s* *am-a-v-erat*	'he/she/it had loved'
1*pl* *am-a-v-eramus*	'we had loved'
2*pl* *am-a-v-eratis*	'you had loved'
3*pl* *am-a-v-erant*	'they had loved'

So: 3rd p.p. + *-eram -eras -erat* (etc.) = pluperfect active, 'I had -ed'.

Pluperfect passive

1*s* *amat-us a um eram*	'I had been loved'
2*s* *amat-us a um eras*	'you had been loved'
3*s* *amat-us a um erat*	'he/she/it had been loved'
1*pl* *amat-i ae a eramus*	'we had been loved'
2*pl* *amat-i ae a eratis*	'you had been loved'
3*pl* *amat-i ae a erant*	'they had been loved'

So: 4th p.p. (*-us a um*) + *eram, eras, erat* (etc.) = pluperfect passive, 'I had been -ed'.

17c Remember: *eram, eras, erat* (etc.) on its own continues to mean 'I was', 'you were', 'he/she/it was' (etc.), as the imperfect of *sum*. Only when blended with other verbs in the way described above does it take on the pluperfect 'had' meaning.

Thus, e.g. *Caesar erat dux*: Caesar was leader; *Caesar Cleopatram amaverat*: Caesar had loved Cleopatra; *Cleopatra a Caesare amata erat*: Cleopatra had been loved by Caesar.

Exercise

N.b. remember how common *a(b)* + abl. (meaning 'by' a person) is in these sentences. Some of last week's new vocabulary will be re-used again here.

Translate: *Pilatus titulum* (title, acc.) *scripserat; titulus a Pilato scriptus erat; ex corde et mente, Pilatus Iesum dimittere voluerat; ubi Pilatus sermonem Iudaeorum audiuit, timebat; pontifices Iudaeorum clamauerant 'crucifige eum!'; Pilatus autem Iesum non dimiserat, sed militibus eum tradiderat; corona capiti eius imposita erat a militibus; Iudaei clamauerant se nullum* ('no') *regem habere nisi Caesarem.*

More passive joys

17d In the pres. and imperf. tenses, we have so far met only active verbs, e.g. 'I love' *amo*, and 'I was loving' *amabam*. But do not these have passives as well, e.g. 'I am being loved' and 'I was being loved'? Of course they do.

17e Trembling, you sense a new set of forms about to descend. Right you are. But remember, Latin is a good, regular language. Taking, therefore, stem + key vowel (yawn), tack on the new passive endings, attempting to restrain your excitement as you do: *-r, -ris, -tur, -mur, -mini, -ntur*. That's it.

17f We exemplify with our old friend the 1st conj. verb *amo*:
(i) in the present: *amo-r* 'I am being loved', *ama-ris* 'you (s) are being loved', *ama-tur* 'he/she/it is being loved', *ama-mur* 'we are being loved', *ama-mini* 'you (*pl*) are being loved', *ama-ntur* 'they are being loved'.
(ii) in the imperfect: *amaba-r* 'I was being loved', *amaba-ris* 'you (s) were being loved', *amaba-tur* 'he/she/it was being loved' (etc.), *amaba-mur, amaba-mini, amaba-ntur*.

17g Those with an inquisitive frame of mind (all of us) will now turn to the *Grammatical Summary*, 26-35, 46-55, to see all five conjugations set out in their full glory, and jolly dull reading they make too (hoorah hoorah), since they are all stem + key vowel + *r, ris, tur* etc., as promised.

Exercise

Check carefully with the *Grammatical Summary* before doing this exercise (especially 3rd, 4th and 5th conj.).

Translate: *portantur, dimittitur, tangebamini, tradimur, quaerebatur, scribitur, ponimini, moneris, accipior, crucifigebaris, incenduntur, regebar, ducitur, capimini, audiebamur*; he is being loved, they were being captured, he is being warned, it was being written, he is being placed, you (*pl*) are being crucified, they were being sought, I am being led, he was being carried.

Translate: *multi milites corpus regis portant; corpus regis a multis militibus portatur; omnes homines palatium incendebant; palatium ab omnibus hominibus incendebatur; Iesus spiritum* (spirit, acc.) *tradidit; spiritus a Iesu traditus est; ubi positum erat corpus Iesu (of Jesus)?; Deus mihi potestatem magnam dat; mihi a Deo potestas magna datur; responsum dabatur discipulis ab omnibus angelis; frater et soror eius ad monumentum missi erant; dum corpus regis miseri portabatur, multi sermones erant; a discipulis miseris corpus in monumento positum erat.*

Answers

17c Pilate had written the title; the title had been written by Pilate; from heart and mind, Pilate had wanted to release Jesus; when Pilate heard the words of the Jews, he was afraid; the leaders of the Jews had shouted 'Crucify him!'; Pilate however had not released Jesus, but (had) handed him over to the soldiers; a crown had been placed on his head by the soldiers; the Jews had cried that they had no king but Caesar.

17g They were being carried, he is being released, you were being touched, we are being handed over, he was being sought, it is being written, you are being placed, you are being warned, I am being received, you were being crucified, they are being burned, I was being ruled, he is being led, you are being captured, we were being heard; *amatur, capiebantur, monetur, scribebatur, ponitur, crucifigimini, quaerebantur, ducor, portabatur.*

Many soldiers carry the body of the king; the body of the king is carried by many soldiers; all the men were burning the palace; the palace was being burnt by all the men; Jesus gave up his spirit; the spirit was given up by Jesus; where had the body of Jesus been placed?; God gives (to) me great power; to me great power is given by God; a reply was being given to the disciples by all the angels; the brother and his sister had been sent to the sepulchre; while the unhappy king's body was being carried, there were many conversations; the body had been placed in the tomb by the unhappy disciples.

The world of Rome

Slavery

In the last chapter we saw how the Roman garrison commander who sent Paul to Rome had originally been a Greek slave.

Slaves were for the most part free people who had been captured in war or by pirates, and sold off in slave markets. It could happen to anyone. A brilliant teacher, say, or superb craftsman would be worth a lot of money and would be well treated by their new owners (why spend the money otherwise?). Educated slaves are known to have risen to high positions in what passed for the civil service at local and government level. It is a sobering thought that some people actually sold themselves into slavery to better themselves: if you had intelligence and training, better to serve a wealthy master as a useful slave than live free but in grinding poverty. For the vicious and brutal, gladiatorial school could be a route to fame and fortune.

At least slaves in the Roman world had the chance to buy their freedom. Indeed, the number of such freedmen exerting influence at the highest level in the emperor's court became a source of some resentment. But the great majority of slaves was purchased simply as work-horses and for them, death was probably a blessed release.

Word play

In previous chapters, we have been looking at the ways in which from the 5th century AD onwards, Latin has infiltrated the basically Germanic English language, thereby enlarging and enriching its vocabulary enormously. But it is worth stepping back briefly now to consider the wider picture, and ask 'where do Germanic languages and Latin themselves come from?'

It is an astonishing fact that the Germanic, Latin, Greek and Sanskrit (north India) languages were all originally the same language. We know this because (i) none of these languages derives from each other, but (ii) they all share a very large number of common roots – so many that it cannot be mere coincidence. Thus, 'father' is in German *Vater*, Latin *pater*, Greek *pater* and Sanskrit *pitar*. 'Mother' is in German *Mutter*, Latin *mater*, Greek *meter* and Sanskrit *matar*. And so on and on and on (German *Fuss*, Latin *pes* and Greek *pous* (foot) is another example).

The only conclusion that stands up is that these languages were all originally the same language, and the people who spoke whatever that language was (we call it Indo-European) split up and moved to different areas, where each language was able to develop independently (rather as Spanish, French and Italian, all Latin-based languages, have done).

So, for example, Germanic *sieben* (giving English 'seven') does not derive from Latin *septem* or Greek *hepta* or Sanskrit *sapta*: it simply shares the same root with them, because they were all originally the same language.

Just to complete the picture, the following language groups are also part of the great Indo-European family: Celtic (giving us Welsh, Cornish, Gaelic and Irish), Slavic (Russian, Polish, Czech, Serbo-Croatian), Indo-Iranian (Hindi, Afghan, Persian) and Albanian.

CHAPTER 18

Nearly there – next chapter, the Bayeux Tapestry and *Carmina Burana*, and after that, some final Catullus and then St John's Easter story. Having therefore come so far, so heroically, you may feel it a mean trick to be asked now, at the eleventh hour, with the prize just round the corner, to be asked to grapple with the subjunctive.

The subjunctive

18a   Let me put your mind at rest. Summon up the blood and take a peek at e.g. *cum* (when) *Caesar venisset, Pompeius miser erat.* OK, you do not know what form *venisset* is, but it obviously comes from *venio* (*ven-*) 'come' and is 3rd *s* (*-t*) and must mean 'When Caesar came, Pompey was unhappy'. You can greet the news that *venisset* is pluperfect subjunctive with glee or resignation, but for translation purposes one cannot honestly say it is a knock-out blow.

Try again: *Caesar, ut* (in order that) *Pompeium vinceret, festinavit ad proelium. vinceret* looks nasty – or does it? *vinc* = 'conquer'; *-t* = 'he' (tee-hee), so 'Caesar, in order that he should/might/conquer Pompey, hurried to battle'. *vinceret* is imperfect subjunctive, but who cares?

The point is that the subjunctive just happens to be used in certain constructions involving *cum* ('when, since') and *ut* ('in order that'). True, the subjunctive is formed differently from the indicative, but we know what sort of language Latin is. The subjunctive still uses the same old stems (so we know what the verb means) and person-endings (so we know who is doing the action) – there are just a few different bits in the middle – so for translation purposes, images of old rope and pieces of cake spring readily to mind.

127

With eye undimmed and carefree brow, then, take a look at three popular constructions using the subjunctive in this way.

cum

18b *cum* meaning 'when/since' is followed by the verb in the subjunctive. Thus *cum puellam amavisset* 'when/since he had loved the girl'; *cum milites a rege ducti essent* 'when/since the soldiers had been led by the king'.

Here the subjunc. has no special meaning in English: Latin just happens to use the subjunc. after *cum*. So you can translate this subjunc. as if it were indicative.

Yes, yes, I know *cum* taking the ablative means 'with'. But is it taking the abl. here? No. Therefore it means 'when/since'. QED. Get on with your exercise.

Exercise

Translate: *rex, cum haec* ('this', acc.) *dixisset, exivit; Iesus, cum acetum* ('vinegar', acc.) *accepisset, spiritum tradidit; Willelm, cum exercitus Haroldi venisset, non timebat; Iesus, cum matrem et discipulum vidisset, dixit matri 'mulier, ecce, filius tuus'; Pilatus, cum sermonem audivisset, timuit.*

ut (i)

18c *ut* meaning 'in order that' puts the verb in the subjunc. Thus: *ut Iesum dimitteret* 'in order that he might release Jesus'; *ut Iesum crucifigerent* 'in order that they might crucify Jesus'.

Exercise

Translate: *milites festinaverunt ut cibum ederent* ('eat'); *Pilatus Iesum tradidit ut crucifigeretur; discipuli venire volebant ut monumentum viderent; Maria redivit ut negaret Iesum in monumento esse.*

ut (ii)

18d *ut* meaning 'that X should –', used after verbs of ordering, warning, advising, persuading (etc.), also puts the verb in the subjunc.

Thus: *Pilatus imperavit ut Iesus dimitteretur* 'Pilate ordered that Jesus should be released'; *Willelm imperat ut milites praeparent se ad proelium* 'William orders that the soldiers should prepare themselves for battle' (or 'the soldiers to prepare themselves').

Exercise

Translate: *moneo ut venias; Harold imperavit ut exercitus mare transiret; cur mihi persuades* ('persuade', + dat.) *ut militem interficiam?; Willelm monuit ut exercitus rediret.*

18e The lesson from all this is that the subjunc. is a piece of cake. If you see a signpost like *cum* or *ut* shouting SUBJUNC. at you, on you go and translate it as it comes, into the most natural English.

Summary

18f Herewith, then, a summary of the main forms of the subjunc.

(i) The subjunc. uses exactly the same stems as the indicatives. Person endings (*-m, -s, -t* etc.) are also all quite regular.

(ii) The present subjunc. is dominated by the letter *-a-* in all conjs. bar the first, where it is dominated by *-e-*. Thus *amo* becomes *amem, ames,* (etc.); *moneo* becomes *moneam, moneas,* (etc.); *rego* becomes *regam;* *audio* becomes *audiam*; and *capio* (yawn) *capiam.*

(iii) In the imperfect subjunc., the person endings are tacked onto the infinitive. Thus, *amare-m amare-s,* (etc.), *monere-m, regere-m, audire-m* and *capere-m.*

(iv) In the pluperfect subjunc., *-issem* is tacked onto the 3rd p.p. Thus *amav-issem, amav-isses,* (etc.), *monu-issem, rex-issem* (must I go on?).

(v) The subjunc. of *sum* is *sim sis sit simus sitis sint;* of *eram* it is *essem esses esset* (go on, finish it off yourself).

See *Grammatical Summary* under the present, imperfect and pluperfect tenses.

Spanner in ointment

18g While the subjunc. is signposted by e.g. *cum* and *ut*, there is no problem. But there is one fly in the works – the present subjunctive can express the idea 'let/may X happen' (the so-called jussive, i.e. 'ordering', subjunctive), and is not signposted: you just have to recognise that the verb is in the subjunc.

Contrast: *amamus* 'we love', *amemus* 'let us love'; *vivimus* 'we live', *vivamus* 'let us live'. So (Catullus):

vivamus, mea Lesbia, atque amemus 'Let us live, my Lesbia, and let us love'.

Compare: *vivit regina* 'the queen is living', *vivat regina* 'let the queen live'; *requiescit in pace* 'he rests in peace', *requiescat in pace* 'let him rest in peace'; *fit lux* 'light is being made', *fiat lux* 'let light be made', 'let there be light' (a fiat is a permission, a 'let it be made/happen'); *habes corpus* 'you have the body', *habeas corpus* 'you may have the body'; *gaudemus* 'we rejoice', *gaudeamus* 'let us rejoice'; *benedictus benedicit* 'the blessed one blesses', *benedictus benedicat* 'may the blessed one bless'.

Exercise

Check *Grammatical Summary* and translate these unsignposted verbs. If they are subjunctive in form, use the 'let/may' form.

veniat; videamus; ament; mittit; ducas; festinemus; respondemus; negant; scribas; ploremus; ponatis; clamatis.

Answers

18b The king, when he had said this, left; Jesus, when he received the vinegar, gave up his spirit; William, when the army of Harold came, was not afraid; Jesus, when he saw his mother and the disciple, said 'Woman, behold, your son'; Pilate, when he heard the conversation, feared.

18c The soldiers hurried in order that they might (= 'to') eat food; Pilate handed over Jesus in order that he might be (= 'to be') crucified; the disciples wished to come in order that they might (= 'to') see the tomb; Mary returned in order that she might deny (= 'to deny') that Jesus was in the tomb.

18d I advise that you come; Harold ordered that the army should cross (= 'to cross') the sea; why do you persuade me that I should kill (= 'to kill') the soldier?; William ordered that the army should return.

18g Let him come; let us see; let them love; he sends; may you lead; let us hurry; we reply; they deny; may you write; let us weep; may you place; you shout.

The world of Rome

Slave makes good

In the last chapter we talked of educated slaves who made good in the emperor's entourage. One of the 50,000 public inscriptions uncovered in Rome is a dedication to one such slave – and what a team he led! Italicised names are Greek:

'To Musicus Scurranus, slave of the emperor Tiberius, chief cashier to the Gallic revenue department (imperial) in the province of Lugdunum (Lyons): some of his team who were with him in Rome when he died set this up to a man who deserved well of them. Venustus, business rep.; *Agathopus*, physician; Facilis, footman; Decimianus, special expenses; *Epaphra*, cashier; *Anthus*, cashier; *Dicaeus*, attendant; Primio, valet; *Hedylus*, chamberlain; Mutatus, attendant; Communis, chamberlain; Firmus, cook; *Creticus*, attendant; *Pothus*, footman; *Tiasus*, cook; Secunda [the only woman].'

Word play

Ancient scientific ideas have thrown up a fascinating range of words that have lost their specific meaning, because the ideas have been discounted, but continue in use for other purposes. Take quintessence – (*quintus* 'fifth', *essentia* 'essence'). Greeks thought there were four basic substances – earth, air, fire and water – but Aristotle postulated a fifth, too ethereal for precise classification. In the Middle Ages this was regarded as the most important substance of all, but when the whole concept of five substances was jettisoned, quintessence survived to mean the most perfect example or purest embodiment of something.

Ancient medical beliefs have given us a rich range of words.

Ancients believed that health was maintained by the balanced mixture in the body of four 'humours' – blood, phlegm, yellow bile and black bile. If the balance was right, you were 'good-humoured'. Absurd behaviour indicated that you had too much of one of these humours – hence 'humorous'. Latin *tempero* means 'mix' and one's *temperamentum* was one's personal 'mixture' of these humours. 'Temper' originally meant the same, before it became associated with anger; 'distemper' meant the mixture had become unbalanced (*dis-* apart, separate). 'Complexion' derives from *cum* ('together') and *plecto* ('weave') – one's temperament, it was believed, was shown by the weaving together of colours in the face. If you had lots of blood (*sanguis*), you were cheerful (sanguine); lots of phlegm, and you were calm and unemotional (phlegmatic).

CHAPTER 19

In the semi-final Latin lesson, we read from the Bayeux tapestry and *Carmina Burana*.

19a Bayeux tapestry
William, Duke of Normandy, has Harold in his power. Harold is made to fight for William in France, and at Bayeux swears an oath of loyalty to the Duke, probably to give him the kingship of England when Edward the Confessor dies. But when Harold returns to England and Edward dies, Harold becomes king. Halley's comet appears. William, claiming he has been betrayed, invades England (1066).

Remember that *hic* means 'here', and refers to the pictures on the tapestry.

Note: *Bagias* to Bayeux; *sacrament-um* oath; *reversus est* returned; *Petr-us* Peter; *lect-us* bed; *alloquitur* addresses; *fideles* (acc.) the faithful; *defunctus est* (he) died; *miro* 1 admire; *aedifico* build; *isti* they, these (nom. *pl*); *carr-us* cart; *navigi-um* ship; *Pevensae* Pevensey; *caball-us* horse; *de* + abl. from, *or* concerning; *Hestinga* to Hastings; *rapio rapere* take; *caro* (nom.) meat; *episcop-us* bishop (Odo); *pot-us* drink; *benedico* 3 bless; *dom-us* house; *iste* he, that man (nom.); *nuntio* 1 inform; *alloquitur suis* orders his ...; *viriliter* bravely; *sapienter* wisely; *qui* (those) who.

hic Willelm dedit Haroldo arma. hic Willelm venit Bagias, ubi Harold sacramentum fecit Willelmo duci. hic Harold dux reversus est ad Anglicam terram, et venit ad Edwardum regem. hic portatur corpus Eadwardi regis ad ecclesiam Sancti Petri Apostoli. hic Eadwardus rex in lecto alloquitur fideles, et hic defunctus est. hic dederunt Haroldo coronam regis. hic residet Harold rex Anglorum. isti mirant stellam.

19b *hic Willelm dux iussit naves (a)edificare. hic trahuntur naves ad mare. isti portant armas ad naves, et hic trahunt carrum cum vino et armis. hic Willelm dux in magno navigio mare transivit et venit ad Pevensae. hic exeunt caballi de navibus, et hic festinaverunt Hestinga ut cibum raperent. hic coquitur caro, et hic ministraverunt ministri. hic fecerunt prandium et hic episcopus cibum et potum benedicit ...*

19c *hic nuntiatum est Willelmo de Haroldo. hic domus incenditur. hic milites exierunt de Hestinga et venerunt ad pr(o)elium contra Haroldum regem. hic Willelm dux interrogat Vital si vidisset exercitum Haroldi. iste nuntiat Haroldum regem de exercitu Wilelmi ducis. hic Willelm dux alloquitur suis militibus ut prepararent se viriliter et sapienter ad pr(o)elium contra Anglorum exercitum ... hic Franci pugnant et ceciderunt qui erant cum Haroldo. hic Harold rex interfectus est, et fuga verterunt Angli.*

19d *Carmina Burana*

This collection of 228 scholars' songs was composed in the 13th century AD and discovered in 1803 in the Bavarian monastery of Benediktbeuern (beuern – *Buranus*). Carl Orff set some of them to music in 1937.

A common theme of the songs is the difficulty the lover has in reassuring the beloved of his constancy. Here the young man announces that his loves transcends time and space – the only way to love truly.

Note: *fideliter* faithfully; *fidem* (acc.) (good) faith; *totaliter* completely; *presantialiter* face to face (with you); *remota* remote (place); *quisquis* whoever; *aliter* any other way; *rota* wheel (i.e. the wheel of torture).

> *ama me fideliter!*
> *fidem meam nota!*
> *de corde totaliter*
> *et ex mente tota*
> *sum presantialiter*
> *absens in remota.*
> *quisquis amat aliter*
> *volvitur in rota.*

19e Here a cygnet bewails its fate. Once it lived beautiful and free, but now it has been cooked and is being served up for dinner.

Note: *lacus* (acc. *pl*) lakes; *exstit-i* I was; *cign-us* cygnet; *ust-us* cooked, burnt; *fortiter* bravely, to a turn; *(re)gir-o* 1 (re)turn; *garcifer* (nom.) chef; *rog-us* fire; *ur-o* cook, burn; *propin-o* serve; *dapifer* steward; *scutell-a* platter; *iaceo* lie; *volito* fly; *nequeo* I am unable; *dens, dent-* tooth; *frendens, frendent-* gnashing.

olim lacus colueram,
olim pulcher exstiteram
dum cignus ego fueram.
miser! miser!
modo niger
et ustus fortiter!

girat, regirat garcifer.
me rogus urit fortiter.
propinat me nunc dapifer.
miser! miser!
modo niger
et ustus fortiter!

nunc in scutella iaceo
et volitare nequeo.
dentes frendentes video.
miser! miser!
modo niger
et ustus fortiter!

Answers

19a Here William gave arms to Harold. Here William came [to] Bayeux, where Harold took an oath to Duke William. Here Duke Harold returned to English territory, and came to King Edward. Here the person of King Edward is carried to the church of St Peter the Apostle. Here King Edward in bed addresses the faithful, and here he is dead. Here they gave Harold the king's crown. Here sits Harold king of the English ...
19b Here William orders [them] to build ships. Here ships are

dragged to the sea. These carry arms to the ships, and here they pull a cart with wine and arms. Here Duke William crosses the sea in a great ship and comes to Pevensey. Here horses leave from the ship, and here they hurry [to] Hastings to get food. Here meat is cooked, and here servants served [it]. Here they made dinner and here the bishop blesses the food and drink …

19c Here it is announced (=an announcement is made) to William about Harold. Here a house is burned. Here soldiers departed from Hastings and came to battle against King Harold. Here Duke William asks Vital if he had seen the army of Harold. That man informs King Harold about the army of Duke William. Here Duke William orders his soldiers that they prepare themselves bravely and wisely for battle against the army of the English … here the French fight and [those] were killed who were with Harold. Here King Harold was killed, and the English turned in flight.

19d Love me truly!/Note my faith!/From [my] heart completely/and from [my] whole mind/I am face-to-face (with you)/(though) absent in a remote [place]./Who loves in any other way/is turned on the wheel.

19e Once I inhabited lakes,/once I had been beautiful/while I had been a cygnet. Unhappy! Unhappy! Now black and done to a turn!

The chef turns and re-turns [me]./The fire cooks me to a turn./The steward now presents me. Unhappy! etc.

Now on the dish I lie/and I cannot fly./I see the gnashing teeth. Unhappy! etc.

Word play

As we have seen (**Word play, Chapter 4**), English received much of its Latinate vocabulary via French after 1066. Naturally, English received it in the form in which it was then current, which did not necessarily bear much relationship to the original Latin. Thus, for example, Latin *fragilis* had become *fraile* in Old French (modern French *frêle*), whence our 'frail'; Latin *fabrica* ('work-shop') became Old French *forge* and so English 'forge'; Latin *redemptio* via Old French *raeçon* became English 'ransom'; and Latin *traditio* ('handing down, handing over') via Old French *traïson* became 'treason'; Latin *species*, Old French *espice*, English 'spice'.

Which leaves the question – what about fragile, fabric, redemption, tradition and species? Where did they come from? The answer is, of course, that they came from Latin. English simply took them over for a second time in a more recognisable Latin form. Why not? No rule against it.

Such words are called etymological doublets. Here's a triplet: Latin *ratio* ('calculation, account, judgement, order, system') gives us, via Old French *raison*, reason; via Middle French *ration*, ration; and directly from Latin, ratio.

CHAPTER 20

In the last Latin lesson, we move from pagan to Christian, from Catullus to St John's Easter story.

20a Catullus and Lesbia

Note: *null-us a um* no; *tant- ... quant-* so much ... as; *se amatam* herself [to have been] loved; *vere* truly; *fides* good faith (nom. f); *ullo ... foedere* in any treaty; *umquam* ever; *in amore tuo* in my love for you; *pars part-* part, side 3f; *reperio 4 repper-i repert-um* find.

> *nulla potest mulier tantum se dicere amatam*
> *vere quantum a me Lesbia amata mea est.*
> *nulla fides ullo fuit umquam foedere tanta*
> *quanta in amore tuo ex parte reperta mea est.*

As usual in such deceptively sophisticated poetry, it is word-order that is the problem. Take it: *nulla mulier potest dicere se vere amatam tantum, quantum mea Lesbia ...; nulla fides umquam fuit tanta ullo foedere, quanta reperta est ... ex mea parte.*

Note that both couplets begin with *nulla* and end with *mea est*. In the second, Catullus tries to define the special nature of the 'true love' he feels for Lesbia – more absolute than a lasting and unconditional pledge. But does he write in triumphant celebration, or despair? Is it all on his side, not hers? Consider especially the last line.

20b From St Jerome's 4th century AD *editio vulgata* ('the Vulgate') of St John's Gospel, chapters 19 and 20.

Greek was the universal language of the eastern Mediterranean from the 3rd century BC onwards. The Old Testament was translated from the Hebrew into Greek in the 3rd century BC (the Septuagint), and Latin translations were made from that (known as 'Old Latin' – *vetus Latina*). Jesus and his disciples spoke a form of Hebrew, but the gospels too were written in simple Greek – they had to be, if the message was to spread.

St Jerome's Latin *editio vulgata* ('the Vulgate', 'popular edition') was based on the existing Greek, Latin and Hebrew versions (St Jerome was a Hebrew scholar too). It was composed in the 4th century AD and was adopted by Charlemagne as the official text of the whole Bible in the 8th century AD. It came to be regarded as the Word of God, and its every syllable was minutely scrutinised and debated by theologians for historical, moral, allegorical and spiritual meaning.

Here we pick up St John's Easter story at the point where Pilate has Jesus flogged.

Note: **19.1-3** *flagello* 1 scourge; *plecto* 3 pluck; *spin-a* thorn; *vest-is* robe 3f; *purpure-us a um* purple; *circum-do dare ded-i* clothe X (acc.) with Y (abl.); *alap-a* blow; **7-12** *secundum* + acc. according to; *mori* to die; *audisset* = *audivisset* (**18d**); *hunc* this (with *sermonem*); *magis* the more; *ingressus est* he entered; *praetorium* judgement hall; *iterum* again; *loqueris* do you speak; *non haberes* you would not have; *adversus* + acc., against; *ullam* any (take with *potestatem*); *datum esset* it had been given; *desuper* from above; *qui* he who; *maius* greater (with *peccatum*); *peccat-um* sin; *exinde* from then on; *hunc* him (acc.); *omnis qui* everyone who; *contradico* contradict (+ dat.); **14-16** *illi* they (nom. *pl*); *crucifigam* shall I crucify?; *illum* him (acc.); **19-22** *titul-us* title; *super* (+ acc.) above; *ipse* he himself; *quod* what; **25-27** *iuxta* + acc. next to; *Iesu* of Jesus; *quem* whom; *suae* his (with *matri*); *deinde* then; **30** *consummo* 1 finish, complete; *inclinato capite* (with) head inclined; **20.11-13** *fleo* 2 weep; *inclinat se* she stoops down; *prospicio* 5 *prospexi* peer, look; *duos* two; *alba* white (clothes); *unum* (acc.) one; *pes ped-* foot; *illi* they (nom. *pl*); *quid* why?; *fero ferre tul-i* remove, take away; **17-18** *nondum* not yet; *enim* for (take as first word); *ascendo* 3 *ascend-i* ascend; *vado* 3 go; *frater fratr-* brother; *annuntio* 1 announce; *haec* this (acc.).

19.1-3 *tunc ergo apprehendit Pilatus Iesum, et flagellavit. et milites, plectentes coronam de spinis, imposuerunt capiti eius: et veste purpurea circumdederunt eum. et veniebant ad eum et dicebant 'ave, rex Iudaeorum'; et dabant ei alapas.*

[Pilate now tells the Jews to crucify Jesus themselves. You read this at **12f.**]

7-12 *responderunt ei Iudaei 'nos legem habemus, et secundum legem debet mori, quia filium Dei se fecit.' cum ergo audisset Pilatus hunc sermonem, magis timuit.*

et ingressus est praetorium iterum, et dixit ad Iesum 'unde es tu?' Iesus autem responsum non dedit ei. dicit ergo ei Pilatus 'mihi non loqueris? nescis quia potestatem habeo crucifigere te, et potestatem habeo dimittere te?' respondit Iesus 'non haberes potestatem adversus me ullam, nisi tibi datum esset desuper. propterea qui me tradidit tibi, maius peccatum habet.'

et exinde quaerebat Pilatus dimittere eum. Iudaei autem clamabant, dicentes 'si hunc dimittis, non est amicus Caesaris. omnis enim qui se regem facit, contradicit Caesari.'

[Pilate takes the tribunal and makes his decision.]

14-16 *et [Pilatus] dicit Iudaeis 'ecce, rex vester'. illi autem clamabant 'tolle, tolle, crucifige eum.' dicit eis Pilatus 'regem vestrum crucifigam?' responderunt pontifices 'non habemus regem nisi Caesarem.' tunc ergo tradidit eis illum ut crucifigeretur.*

[Jesus is taken out and crucified.]

19-22 *scripsit autem et titulum Pilatus, et posuit super crucem. erat autem scriptum 'Iesus Nazarenus, rex Iudaeorum' … dicebant ergo Pilato pontifices Iudaeorum 'noli scribere "rex Iudaeorum", sed quia ipse dixit "rex sum Iudaeorum"'. respondit Pilatus 'quod scripsi, scripsi'.*

[Jesus' clothing is divided up.]

25-27 *stabant autem iuxta crucem Iesu mater eius, et soror matris eius, Maria Cleophae et Maria Magdalene. cum vidisset ergo Iesus matrem, et discipulum stantem, quem diligebat, dicit matri suae 'mulier, ecce, filius tuus'. deinde dicit discipulo 'ecce, mater tua'.*

[Jesus is given vinegar (*acetum*).]

30 *cum ergo accepisset Iesus acetum, dixit 'consummatum est'. et inclinato capite, tradidit spiritum.*

[Mary, having found the tomb empty and after telling the disciples, stands there weeping.]

20.11-13 *Maria autem stabat ad monumentum plorans. dum ergo fleret, inclinavit se, et prospexit in monumentum. et vidit duos angelos in albis, sedentes, unum ad caput et unum ad pedes, ubi positum fuerat corpus Iesu. dicunt ei illi 'mulier, quid ploras?' dicit eis 'quia tulerunt Dominum meum, et nescio ubi posuerunt eum'.*

[Jesus appears and Mary recognises him.]

17-18 *dicit ei Iesus 'noli me tangere. nondum enim ascendi ad Patrem meum. vade autem ad fratres meos, et dic eis 'ascendo ad Patrem meum, et Patrem vestrum, Deum meum et Deum vestrum'. venit Maria Magdalene, annuntians discipulis quia 'vidi Dominum, et haec mihi dixit'.*

Answers

20a No woman can say she has been truly loved so much as my Lesbia has been loved by me; no good faith was ever found so much in any treaty, as was found in my love for you from my part.
20b Consult your Bible.

Word play

Let us end with the king of the gods.

One of the most extraordinary words in ancient Greek is the name of Zeus. He is in fact *Sdeus* (Greek *z* was pronounced *sd-*), the stem of which is *diw-*, and he is etymologically connected with the Indic god Dyaus pita. This *dyau-/diw-* root means brightness, resplendence, and they are both gods of the sky (remember Zeus as god of the storm, and his thunderbolts). *Sdeus* emerges in Latin as *deus; Dyaus pita* emerges as *Diespiter*, father (*pater*) of the day (*dies*) – whence Jupiter. The *div-*

stem in Latin yields *divinus* and *Diana*; *dies* 'day' yields *diarium* (whence 'diary', which you keep every day) and *diurnus* ('daily') which, through French, emerges into English as 'journal'.

So when you read your journals and keep your diary, reflect that, linguistically at any rate, you are dealing with the great king of the ancient gods.

Scansion

Poetry in English should rhyme, scan and make sense. Latin poetry does not rhyme, does scan and often makes sense.

1. For purposes of scansion in Latin, every syllable counts. Each syllable must scan long (–) or short (∪).

2. The four Catullus poems you have read are written in what are called elegiac couplets. The feet of this metre are the dactyl (–∪∪ tum titi) and spondee (– – tum tum).

3. The first line of the couplet scans as a hexameter (i.e. it has six of these feet), the second (indented in your text) as a pentameter (i.e. with five of these feet, or rather two x two-and-a-half feet).

4. The hexameter scans:

First four feet: dactyls or spondees: fifth foot dactyl: sixth foot – – or –∪.

5. the pentameter scans:

First two feet: dactyls or spondees or spondees: then a long or short syllable: then two dactyls: then a long or short syllable.

The rules for determining long or short syllables are complex. For your purposes, note that a word ending in a vowel or *-um* loses that syllable if the next word begins with a vowel ('elision'). Such elision has been marked with a - in the poems below.

Basically, think belly-dancer. Think tum-titi and tum-tum.

Chapter 14

14a ōd- ĕt ămo. quar- ĭd făcĭam, fortasse rĕquīris.

nĕsciŏ, sed fĭĕri sentĭ- ĕt excrŭcĭor.

14b nulli sē dicit mŭlĭer mĕā nŭbĕre malle

quam mĭhĭ, non si se Iuppĭter ipse pĕtat.

dicit: sed mulier cupido quod dicit amanti,

in vent- et rapida scriber- oportet aqua.

Chapter 16

Quintia formos- est multis; mihi candida, longa,

rect- est: so these individual points I admit.

tot- illud 'formosa' nego: nam nulla venustas,

null- in tam magn- est corpore mica salis.

Lesbia formos- est, quae, cum pulcherrima tot- est,

and second, on her own robs all the others of their
charms.

Chapter 20

nulla potest mulier tantum se dicer- amatam

vere quant- a me Lesbi- amata me- est.

nulla fides ullo fuit umquam foedere tanta

quant- in amore tu- ex parte reperta me- est.

GRAMMATICAL SUMMARY

VERBS

THE FIVE CONJUGATIONS

Note: references in italicised brackets [*(1B)*, etc.] are to chapter sections.

PRESENT ACTIVE

First conjugation
1   Indicative *(1B)*

1s	am-o	'I love, I do love, I am loving'
2s	am-a-s	'you love, you do love, you are loving' (singular)
3s	am-a-t	'he/she/it loves, does love (etc.)'
1pl	am-a-mus	'we love (etc.)'
2pl	am-a-tis	'you love (etc.)' (plural)
3pl	am-a-nt	'they love (etc.)'

2   Infinitive *(1B)*
    am-a-re   'to love'
3   Imperative *(7A)*
    am-a (s) am-a-te (pl) 'love!'
4   Participle *(12F)*
    am-ans amant- (3 adj.) 'loving'
5   Subjunctive *(18)*

1s	am-e-m
2s	am-e-s
3s	am-e-t
1pl	am-e-mus
2pl	am-e-tis
3pl	am-e-nt

Second conjugation
6   Indicative *(2B)*

145

	1s	mon-e-o	'I warn, am warning, do warn'
	2s	mon-e-s	
	3s	mon-e-t	
	1pl	mon-e-mus	
	2pl	mon-e-tis	
	3pl	mon-e-nt	

7 <u>Infinitive *(2B)*</u>
mon-e-re 'to warn'
8 <u>Imperative *(7A)*</u>
mon-e (s) mon-e-te (pl) 'warn!'
9 <u>Participle *(12F)*</u>
mon-ens monent- (3 adj.) 'warning'
10 <u>Subjunctive *(18)*</u>

	1s	mon-ea-m
	2s	mon-ea-s
	3s	mon-ea-t
	1pl	mon-ea-mus
	2pl	mon-ea-tis
	3pl	mon-ea-nt

Third conjugation
11 <u>Indicative *(2D)*</u>

	1s	reg-o	'I rule, do rule, am ruling'
	2s	reg-i-s	
	3s	reg-i-t	
	1pl	reg-i-mus	
	2pl	reg-i-tis	
	3pl	reg-u-nt	

12 <u>Infinitive *(2D)*</u>
reg-e-re 'to rule'
13 <u>Imperative *(7A)*</u>
reg-e (s) reg-i-te (pl) 'rule!'
14 <u>Participle *(12F)*</u>
reg-ens regent- (3 adj.) 'ruling'
15 <u>Subjunctive *(18)*</u>

	1s	reg-a-m
	2s	reg-a-s
	3s	reg-a-t
	1pl	reg-a-mus
	2pl	reg-a-tis
	3pl	reg-a-nt

Fourth conjugation
16 <u>Indicative *(2F)*</u>

	1s	aud-i-o	'I hear, am hearing, do hear'
	2s	aud-i-s	
	3s	aud-i-t	

146

  1pl aud-i-mus
  2pl aud-i-tis
  3pl aud-i-unt
17 <u>Infinitive *(2F)*</u>
  aud-i-re   'to hear'
18 <u>Imperative *(7A)*</u>
  aud-i (s) aud-i-te (pl) 'hear!'
19 <u>Participle *(12F)*</u>
  aud-iens audient- (3 adj.) 'hearing'
20 <u>Subjunctive *(18)*</u>
   1s aud-ia-m
   2s aud-ia-s
   3s aud-ia-t
   1pl aud-ia-mus
   2pl aud-ia-tis
   3pl aud-ia-nt

Fifth conjugation

21 <u>Indicative *(2H)*</u>
   1s cap-i-o   'I capture, am capturing, do capture'
   2s cap-i-s
   3s cap-i-t
   1pl cap-i-mus
   2pl cap-i-tis
   3pl cap-i-unt
22 <u>Infinitive *(2H)*</u>
  cap-e-re   'to capture'
23 <u>Imperative *(7A)*</u>
  cap-e (s) cap-i-te (pl) 'capture!'
24 <u>Participle *(12F)*</u>
  cap-iens capient- (3 adj.) 'capturing'
25 <u>Subjunctive *(18)*</u>
   1s cap-ia-m
   2s cap-ia-s
   3s cap-ia-t
   1pl cap-ia-mus
   2pl cap-ia-tis
   3pl cap-ia-nt

PRESENT PASSIVE

First conjugation

26 <u>Indicative *(17D)*</u>
   1s am-o-r   'I am (being) loved'
   2s am-a-ris 'you (s) are (being) loved'
   3s am-a-tur 'he/she/it is (being) loved'
   1pl am-a-mur 'we are (being) loved'

	2pl	am-a-mini	'you (pl) are (being) loved'
	3pl	am-a-ntur	'they are (being) loved'
27	Subjunctive *(18)*		
	1s	am-e-r	
	2s	am-e-ris	
	3s	am-e-tur	
	1pl	am-e-mur	
	2pl	am-e-mini	
	3pl	am-e-ntur	

Second conjugation

28	Indicative *(17D)*		
	1s	mon-e-or	'I am (being) warned', etc.
	2s	mon-e-ris	
	3s	mon-e-tur	
	1pl	mon-e-mur	
	2pl	mon-e-mini	
	3pl	mon-e-ntur	
29	Subjunctive *(18)*		
	1s	mon-ea-r	
	2s	mon-ea-ris	
	3s	mon-ea-tur	
	1pl	mon-ea-mur	
	2pl	mon-ea-mini	
	3pl	mon-ea-ntur	

Third conjugation

30	Indicative *(17D)*		
	1s	reg-or	'I am (being) ruled', etc.
	2s	reg-e-ris	
	3s	reg-i-tur	
	1pl	reg-i-mur	
	2pl	reg-i-mini	
	3pl	reg-u-ntur	
31	Subjunctive *(18)*		
	1s	reg-a-r	
	2s	reg-a-ris	
	3s	reg-a-tur	
	1pl	reg-a-mur	
	2pl	reg-a-mini	
	3pl	reg-a-ntur	

Fourth conjugation

32	Indicative *(17D)*		
	1s	aud-i-or	'I am (being) heard', etc.
	2s	aud-i-ris	
	3s	aud-i-tur	

	1pl	aud-i-mur
	2pl	aud-i-mini
	3pl	aud-i-untur
33	Subjunctive *(18)*	
	1s	aud-ia-r
	2s	aud-ia-ris
	3s	aud-ia-tur
	1pl	aud-ia-mur
	2pl	aud-ia-mini
	3pl	aud-ia-ntur

Fifth conjugation

34	Indicative *(17D)*		
	1s	cap-i-or	'I am (being) captured', etc.
	2s	cap-e-ris	
	3s	cap-i-tur	
	1pl	cap-i-mur	
	2pl	cap-i-mini	
	3pl	cap-i-untur	
35	Subjunctive *(18)*		
	1s	cap-ia-r	
	2s	cap-ia-ris	
	3s	cap-ia-tur	
	1pl	cap-ia-mur	
	2pl	cap-ia-mini	
	3pl	cap-ia-ntur	

IMPERFECT ACTIVE

First conjugation

36	Indicative *(11A)*		
	1s	am-a-ba-m	'I was loving, used to love'
	2s	am-a-ba-s	'you were loving, used to love'
	3s	am-a-ba-t	'he/she/it was loving, used to love'
	1pl	am-a-ba-mus	'we were loving, used to love'
	2pl	am-a-ba-tis	'you were loving, used to love
	3pl	am-a-ba-nt	'they were loving, used to love'
37	Subjunctive *(18)*		
	1s	am-a-re-m	
	2s	am-a-re-s	
	3s	am-a-re-t	
	1pl	am-a-re-mus	
	2pl	am-a-re-tis	
	3pl	am-a-re-nt	

Second conjugation

38 <u>Indicative *(11A)*</u>

1s	mon-e-ba-m	'I was warning, used to warn', etc.
2s	mon-e-ba-s	
3s	mon-e-ba-t	
1pl	mon-e-ba-mus	
2pl	mon-e-ba-tis	
3pl	mon-e-ba-nt	

39 <u>Subjunctive *(18)*</u>

1s	mon-e-re-m
2s	mon-e-re-s
3s	mon-e-re-t
1pl	mon-e-re-mus
2pl	mon-e-re-tis
3pl	mon-e-re-nt

Third conjugation

40 <u>Indicative *(11A)*</u>

1s	reg-e-ba-m	'I was ruling, used to rule', etc.
2s	reg-e-ba-s	
3s	reg-e-ba-t	
1pl	reg-e-ba-mus	
2pl	reg-e-ba-tis	
3pl	reg-e-ba-nt	

41 <u>Subjunctive *(18)*</u>

1s	reg-e-re-m
2s	reg-e-re-s
3s	reg-e-re-t
1pl	reg-e-re-mus
2pl	reg-e-re-tis
3pl	reg-e-re-nt

Fourth conjugation

42 <u>Indicative *(11A)*</u>

1s	aud-i-e-ba-m	'I was hearing, used to hear', etc.
2s	aud-i-e-ba-s	
3s	aud-i-e-ba-t	
1pl	aud-i-e-ba-mus	
2pl	aud-i-e-ba-tis	
3pl	aud-i-e-ba-nt	

43 <u>Subjunctive *(18)*</u>

1s	aud-i-re-m
2s	aud-i-re-s
3s	aud-i-re-t
1pl	aud-i-re-mus
2pl	aud-i-re-tis
3pl	aud-i-re-nt

Fifth conjugation

44 <u>Indicative *(11A)*</u>

1s	cap-i-e-ba-m	'I was capturing, used to capture', etc.
2s	cap-i-e-ba-s	
3s	cap-i-e-ba-t	
1pl	cap-i-e-ba-mus	
2pl	cap-i-e-ba-tis	
3pl	cap-i-e-ba-nt	

45 <u>Subjunctive *(18)*</u>

1s	cap-e-re-m
2s	cap-e-re-s
3s	cap-e-re-t
1pl	cap-e-re-mus
2pl	cap-e-re-tis
3pl	cap-e-re-nt

IMPERFECT PASSIVE

First conjugation

46 <u>Indicative *(17F)*</u>

1s	am-a-ba-r	'I was being loved'
2s	am-a-ba-ris	'you were being loved'
3s	am-a-ba-tur	'he/she/it was being loved'
1pl	am-a-ba-mur	'we were being loved'
2pl	am-a-ba-mini	'you were being loved'
3pl	am-a-ba-ntur	'they were being loved'

47 <u>Subjunctive *(18)*</u>

1s	am-a-re-r
2s	am-a-re-ris
3s	am-a-re-tur
1pl	am-a-re-mur
2pl	am-a-re-mini
3pl	am-a-re-ntur

Second conjugation

48 <u>Indicative *(17F)*</u>

1s	mon-e-ba-r	'I was being warned', etc.
2s	mon-e-ba-ris	
3s	mon-e-ba-tur	
1pl	mon-e-ba-mur	
2pl	mon-e-ba-mini	
3pl	mon-e-ba-ntur	

49 <u>Subjunctive *(18)*</u>

1s	mon-e-re-r
2s	mon-e-re-ris
3s	mon-e-re-tur
1pl	mon-e-re-mur

2pl   mon-e-re-mini
3pl   mon-e-re-ntur

Third conjugation
50   Indicative *(17F)*
   1s   reg-e-ba-r   'I was being ruled', etc.
   2s   reg-e-ba-ris
   3s   reg-e-ba-tur
   1pl reg-e-ba-mur
   2pl reg-e-ba-mini
   3pl reg-e-ba-ntur
51   Subjunctive *(18)*
   1s   reg-e-re-r
   2s   reg-e-re-ris
   3s   reg-e-re-tur
   1pl reg-e-re-mur
   2pl reg-e-re-mini
   3pl reg-e-re-ntur

Fourth conjugation
52   Indicative *(17F)*
   1s   aud-i-e-ba-r   'I was being heard', etc.
   2s   aud-i-e-ba-ris
   3s   aud-i-e-ba-tur
   1pl aud-i-e-ba-mur
   2pl aud-i-e-ba-mini
   3pl aud-i-e-ba-ntur
53   Subjunctive *(18)*
   1s   aud-i-re-r
   2s   aud-i-re-ris
   3s   aud-i-re-tur
   1pl aud-i-re-mur
   2pl aud-i-re-mini
   3pl aud-i-re-ntur

Fifth conjugation
54   Indicative *(17F)*
   1s   cap-i-e-ba-r   'I was being captured', etc.
   2s   cap-i-e-ba-ris
   3s   cap-i-e-ba-tur
   1pl cap-i-e-ba-mur
   2pl cap-i-e-ba-mini
   3pl cap-i-e-ba-ntur
55   Subjunctive *(18)*
   1s   cap-e-re-r
   2s   cap-e-re-ris
   3s   cap-e-re-tur

1pl	cap-e-re-mur
2pl	cap-e-re-mini
3pl	cap-e-re-ntur

PERFECT ACTIVE

First conjugation
56 Indicative *(12A)*

1s	am-a-v-i	'I (have) loved, did love'
2s	am-a-v-isti	'you (have) loved, did love'
3s	am-a-v-it	'he/she/it (has) loved, did love'
1pl	am-a-v-imus	'we (have) loved, did love'
2pl	am-a-v-istis	'you (have) loved, did love'
3pl	am-a-v-erunt	'they (have) loved, did love'

Second conjugation
57 Indicative *(12C)*

1s	mon-u-i	'I (have) warned, did warn'
2s	mon-u-isti	
3s	mon-u-it	
1pl	mon-u-imus	
2pl	mon-u-istis	
3pl	mon-u-erunt	

Third conjugation
58 Indicative *(8D)*
Note: the 3rd p.p.s of third conjugation verbs are all irregular: they have to be known.

1s	rex-i	'I (have) ruled, did rule'
2s	rex-isti	
3s	rex-it	
1pl	rex-imus	
2pl	rex-istis	
3pl	rex-erunt	

Fourth conjugation
59 Indicative *(12D)*

1s	aud-i-v-i	'I (have) heard, did hear'
2s	aud-i-v-isti	
3s	aud-i-v-it	
1pl	aud-i-v-imus	
2pl	aud-i-v-istis	
3pl	aud-i-v-erunt	

Fifth conjugation
60 Indicative *(8D)*
Note: the 3rd p.p.s of 5th conj. verbs are all irregular: they have to be known.

1s	cep-i	'I (have) captured, did capture'
2s	cep-isti	
3s	cep-it	
1pl	cep-imus	
2pl	cep-istis	
3pl	cep-erunt	

PERFECT PASSIVE

First conjugation
61 Indicative *(14H)*

1s	amat-us a um sum	'I was, have been loved'
2s	amat-us a um es	'you were, have been loved
3s	amat-us a um est	'he/she/it was, has been loved'
1pl	amat-i ae a sumus	'we were, have been loved'
2pl	amat-i ae a estis	'you were, have been loved'
3pl	amat-i ae a sunt	'they were, have been loved'

Second conjugation
62 Indicative *(14H)*

1s	monit-us a um sum	'I was, have been warned'
2s	monit-us a um es	
3s	monit-us a um est	
1pl	monit-i ae a sumus	
2pl	monit-i ae a estis	
3pl	monit-i ae a sunt	

Third conjugation
63 Indicative *(14H)*

1s	rect-us a um sum	'I was, have been ruled'
2s	rect-us a um es	
3s	rect-us a um est	
1pl	rect-i ae a sumus	
2pl	rect-i ae a estis	
3pl	rect-i ae a sunt	

Fourth conjugation
64 Indicative *(14H)*

1s	audit-us a um sum	'I was, have been heard'
2s	audit-us a um es	
3s	audit-us a um est	
1pl	audit-i ae a sumus	
2pl	audit-i ae a estis	
3pl	audit-i ae a sunt	

Fifth conjugation
65 <u>Indicative <i>(14H)</i></u>

1s	capt-us a um sum	'I was, have been captured'
2s	capt-us a um es	
3s	capt-us a um est	
1pl	capt-i ae a sumus	
2pl	capt-i ae a estis	
3pl	capt-i ae a sunt	

PLUPERFECT ACTIVE

First conjugation
66 <u>Indicative <i>(17B)</i></u>

1s	am-a-v-eram	'I had loved'
2s	am-a-v-eras	'you had loved'
3s	am-a-v-erat	'he/she/it had loved'
1pl	am-a-v-eramus	'we had loved'
2pl	am-a-v-eratis	'you had loved'
3pl	am-a-v-erant	'they had loved'

67 <u>Subjunctive <i>(18)</i></u>

1s	am-a-v-issem
2s	am-a-v-isses
3s	am-a-v-isset
1pl	am-a-v-issemus
2pl	am-a-v-issetis
3pl	am-a-v-issent

Second conjugation
68 <u>Indicative <i>(17B)</i></u>

1s	mon-u-eram	'I had warned'
2s	mon-u-eras	
3s	mon-u-erat	
1pl	mon-u-eramus	
2pl	mon-u-eratis	
3pl	mon-u-erant	

69 <u>Subjunctive <i>(18)</i></u>

1s	mon-u-issem
2s	mon-u-isses
3s	mon-u-isset
1pl	mon-u-issemus
2pl	mon-u-issetis
3pl	mon-u-issent

Third conjugation
70 <u>Indicative <i>(17B)</i></u>

Note: the 3rd p.p.s of third conjugation verbs are all irregular: they have to be known.

1s	rex-eram	'I had ruled'
2s	rex-eras	
3s	rex-erat	
1pl	rex-eramus	
2pl	rex-eratis	
3pl	rex-erant	

71 <u>Subjunctive *(18)*</u>

1s	rex-issem
2s	rex-isses
3s	rex-isset
1pl	rex-issemus
2pl	rex-issetis
3pl	rex-issent

Fourth conjugation
72 <u>Indicative *(17B)*</u>

1s	aud-i-v-eram	'I had heard'
2s	aud-i-v-eras	
3s	aud-i-v-erat	
1pl	aud-i-v-eramus	
2pl	aud-i-v-eratis	
3pl	aud-i-v-erant	

73 <u>Subjunctive *(18)*</u>

1s	aud-i-v-issem
2s	aud-i-v-isses
3s	aud-i-v-isset
1pl	aud-i-v-issemus
2pl	aud-i-v-issetis
3pl	aud-i-v-issent

Fifth conjugation
74 <u>Indicative *(7B)*</u>
Note: the 3rd p.p.s of fifth conjugation verbs are all irregular: they have to be known.

1s	cep-eram	'I had captured'
2s	cep-eras	
3s	cep-erat	
1pl	cep-eramus	
2pl	cep-eratis	
3pl	cep-erant	

75 <u>Subjunctive *(18)*</u>

1s	cep-issem
2s	cep-isses
3s	cep-isset
1pl	cep-issemus
2pl	cep-issetis
3pl	cep-issent

PLUPERFECT PASSIVE
First conjugation
76 <u>Indicative <i>(17B)</i></u>

1s	amat-us a um eram	'I had been loved'
2s	amat-us a um eras	'you had been loved'
3s	amat-us a um erat	'he/she/it had been loved'
1pl	amat-i ae a eramus	'we had been loved'
2pl	amat-i ae a eratis	'you had been loved'
3pl	amat-i ae a erant	'they had been loved'

77 <u>Subjunctive <i>(18)</i></u>

1s	amat-us a um essem
2s	amat-us a um esses
3s	amat-us a um esset
1pl	amat-i ae a essemus
2pl	amat-i ae a essestis
3pl	amat-i ae a essent

Second conjugation
78 <u>Indicative <i>(17B)</i></u>

1s	monit-us a um eram	'I had been warned'
2s	monit-us a um eras	
3s	monit-us a um erat	
1pl	monit-i ae a eramus	
2pl	monit-i ae a eratis	
3pl	monit-i ae a erant	

79 <u>Subjunctive <i>(18)</i></u>

1s	monit-us a um essem
2s	monit-us a um esses
3s	monit-us a um esset
1pl	monit-i ae a essemus
2pl	monit-i ae a essestis
3pl	monit-i ae a essent

Third conjugation
80 <u>Indicative (17B)</u>

1s	rect-us a um eram	'I had been ruled'
2s	rect-us a um eras	
3s	rect-us a um erat	
1pl	rect-i ae a eramus	
2pl	rect-i ae a eratis	
3pl	rect-i ae a erant	

81 <u>Subjunctive <i>(18)</i></u>

1s	rect-us a um essem
2s	rect-us a um esses
3s	rect-us a um esset
1pl	rect-i ae a essemus
2pl	rect-i ae a essestis

3pl   rect-i ae a essent

Fourth conjugation

82 <u>Indicative *(17B)*</u>

1s	audit-us a um eram 'I had been heard'
2s	audit-us a um eras
3s	audit-us a um erat
1pl	audit-i ae a eramus
2pl	audit-i ae a eratis
3pl	audit-i ae a erant

83 <u>Subjunctive *(18)*</u>

1s	audit-us a um essem
2s	audit-us a um esses
3s	audit-us a um esset
1pl	audit-i ae a essemus
2pl	audit-i ae a essestis
3pl	audit-i ae a essent

Fifth conjugation

84 <u>Indicative *(17B)*</u>

1s	capt-us a um eram 'I had been captured'
2s	capt-us a um eras
3s	capt-us a um erat
1pl	capt-i ae a eramus
2pl	capt-i ae a eratis
3pl	capt-i ae a erant

85 <u>Subjunctive *(18)*</u>

1s	capt-us a um essem
2s	capt-us a um esses
3s	capt-us a um esset
1pl	capt-i ae a essemus
2pl	capt-i ae a essestis
3pl	capt-i ae a essent

IRREGULAR VERBS

e-o i-re iv-i it-um 'I go'

PRESENT

86 <u>Indicative *(10E)*</u>

1s	eo 'I go'
2s	i-s
3s	i-t
1pl	i-mus
2pl	i-tis
3pl	e-unt

87 <u>Infinitive *(10E)*</u>

i-re   'to go'
88 <u>Imperative <i>(10E)</i></u>
    i (s) ite (pl)   'go!'

IMPERFECT

89 <u>Indicative <i>(11B)</i></u>
    1s   i-bam   'I was going'
    2s   i-bas
    3s   i-bat
    1pl   i-bamus
    2pl   i-batis
    3pl   i-bant

PERFECT

90 <u>Indicative <i>(10E)</i></u>
    1s   i(v)-i   'I went, have gone'
    2s   i(v)-isti
    3s   i(v)-it
    1pl   i(v)-imus
    2pl   i(v)-istis
    3pl   i(v)-erunt

PLUPERFECT

91 <u>Indicative <i>(17B)</i></u>
    1s   i(v)-eram   'I had gone'
    2s   i(v)-eras
    3s   i(v)-erat
    1pl   i(v)-eramus
    2pl   i(v)-eratis
    3pl   i(v)-erant

pos-sum (=pot-sum) posse potu-i 'I can, am able'

PRESENT

92 <u>Indicative <i>(5D)</i></u>
    1s   possum   'I am able, I can'
    2s   potes
    3s   potest
    1pl   possumus
    2pl   potestis
    3pl   possunt
93 <u>Infinitive <i>(5D)</i></u>
    posse   'to be able'

159

94 Subjunctive *(18)*
    1s   possim
    2s   possis
    3s   possit
    1pl possimus
    2pl possitis
    3pl possint

IMPERFECT

95 Indicative *(11B)*
    1s   poteram   'I was able, could'
    2s   poteras
    3s   poterat
    1pl poteramus
    2pl poteratis
    3pl poterant
96 Subjunctive *(18)*
    1s   posse-m
    2s   posse-s
    3s   posse-t
    1pl posse-mus
    2pl posse-tis
    3pl posse-nt

PERFECT

97 Indicative *(8D)*
    1s   potu-i   'I was able, could'
    2s   potu-isti
    3s   potu-it
    1pl potu-imus
    2pl potu-istis
    3pl potu-erunt

PLUPERFECT

98 Indicative *(17B)*
    1s   potu-eram   'I had been able'
    2s   potu-eras
    3s   potu-erat
    1pl potu-eramus
    2pl potu-eratis
    3pl potu-erant
99 Subjunctive *(18)*
    1s   potu-issem
    2s   potu-isses

3s	potu-isset
1pl	potu-issemus
2pl	potu-issetis
3pl	potu-issent

sum esse fui 'I am'

PRESENT

100 <u>Indicative *(4E)*</u>
1s	sum	'I am'
2s	es	
3s	est	
1pl	sumus	
2pl	estis	
3pl	sunt	

101 <u>Infinitive *(4E)*</u>
| esse | 'to be' |

102 <u>Subjunctive *(18)*</u>
1s	sim
2s	sis
3s	sit
1pl	simus
2pl	sitis
3pl	sint

IMPERFECT

103 <u>Indicative *(11B)*</u>
1s	eram	'I was'
2s	eras	
3s	erat	
1pl	eramus	
2pl	eratis	
3pl	erant	

104 <u>Subjunctive *(18)*</u>
1s	esse-m
2s	esse-s
3s	esse-t
1pl	esse-mus
2pl	esse-tis
3pl	esse-nt

PERFECT

105 <u>Indicative *(8D)*</u>
| 1s | fu-i | 'I was, have been' |

2s	fu-isti
3s	fu-it
1pl	fu-imus
2pl	fu-istis
3pl	fu-erunt

PLUPERFECT

106 <u>Indicative *(17B)*</u>

1s	fu-eram	'I had been'
2s	fu-eras	
3s	fu-erat	
1pl	fu-eramus	
2pl	fu-eratis	
3pl	fu-erant	

107 <u>Subjunctive *(18)*</u>

1s	fu-issem
2s	fu-isses
3s	fu-isset
1pl	fu-issemus
2pl	fu-issetis
3pl	fu-issent

volo velle volu-i 'I wish, want' *(13A)*

PRESENT

108 <u>Indicative</u>

1s	volo	'I wish'
2s	vis	
3s	vult	
1pl	volumus	
2pl	vultis	
3pl	volunt	

109 <u>Infinitive</u>

velle	'to wish'

IMPERFECT

110 <u>Indicative</u>

1s	volebam	'I was wishing'
2s	volebas	
3s	volebat	
1pl	volebamus	
2pl	volebatis	
3pl	volebant	

PERFECT

111 <u>Indicative</u>
    volu-i   'I wished, have wished'

PLUPERFECT

112 <u>Indicative</u>
    volu-eram   'I had wished'

nolo nolle nolu-i 'I refuse, do not want, wish' *(13A)*

PRESENT

113 <u>Indicative</u>
    1s   nolo   'I refuse'
    2s   non vis
    3s   non vult
    1pl   nolumus
    2pl   non vultis
    3pl   nolunt
114 <u>Infinitive</u>
    nolle   'to refuse'
115 <u>Imperative *(5E)*</u>
    noli (s), nolite (pl)   'don't!'

IMPERFECT

116 <u>Indicative</u>
    1s   nolebam   'I was refusing'
    2s   nolebas
    3s   nolebat
    1pl   nolebamus
    2pl   nolebatis
    3pl   nolebant

PERFECT

117 <u>Indicative</u>
    nolu-i   'I refused, have refused'

PLUPERFECT

118 <u>Indicative</u>
    nolu-eram   'I had refused'

malo malle malu-i 'I prefer' *(13A)*

163

PRESENT

119 <u>Indicative</u>
    1s   malo   'I prefer'
    2s   mavis
    3s   mavult
    1pl   malumus
    2pl   mavultis
    3pl   malunt
120 <u>Infinitive</u>
    malle   'to wish'

IMPERFECT

121 <u>Indicative</u>
    1s   malebam   'I was preferring'
    2s   malebas
    3s   malebat
    1pl   malebamus
    2pl   malebatis
    3pl   malebant

PERFECT

122 <u>Indicative</u>
    malu-i   'I preferred, have preferred'

PLUPERFECT

123 <u>Indicative</u>
    malu-eram   'I had preferred'

NOUNS

THE THREE MAIN DECLENSIONS

124 FIRST DECLENSION (f)

<u>Singular</u> *(3B, 10B)*
nom. serv-a
voc.   serv-a
acc.   serv-am
gen.   serv-ae
dat.   serv-ae
abl.   serv-a

Plural *(7B, 10B)*

nom.	serv-ae
voc.	serv-ae
acc.	serv-as
gen.	serv-arum
dat.	serv-is
abl.	serv-is

125 SECOND DECLENSION (m)

Singular *(4A, 10C)*

nom.	serv-us
voc.	serv-e
acc.	serv-um
gen.	serv-i
dat.	serv-o
abl.	serv-o

Plural *(7B, 10C)*

nom.	serv-i
voc.	serv-i
acc.	serv-os
gen.	serv-orum
dat.	serv-is
abl.	serv-is

126 SECOND DECLENSION (n)

Singular *(4A)*

nom.	bell-um
voc.	bell-um
acc.	bell-um
gen.	bell-i
dat.	bell-o
abl.	bell-o

Plural *(10C)*

nom.	bell-a
voc.	bell-a
acc.	bell-a
gen.	bell-orum
dat.	bell-is
abl.	bell-is

127 THIRD DECLENSION (m, f)

Singular *(6C, 10D)*
nom. dux
voc. dux
acc. duc-em
gen. duc-is
dat. duc-i
abl. duc-e

Plural *(7B)*
nom. duc-es
voc. duc-es
acc. duc-es
gen. duc-um
dat. duc-ibus
abl. duc-ibus

128 THIRD DECLENSION (n) *(16B)*

Singular
nom. corpus
voc. corpus
acc. corpus
gen. corpor-is
dat. corpor-i
abl. corpor-e

Plural
nom. corpor-a
voc. corpor-a
acc. corpor-a
gen. corpor-um
dat. corpor-ibus
abl. corpor-ibus

NOTE: you will find third declension nouns with abl. s in -i and gen. pl in -ium.

PRONOUNS (9B)

129 ego/nos 'I-me/we-us'

Singular
nom. ego
acc. me
gen. mei
dat. mihi
abl. me

Plural

nom.	nos
acc.	nos
gen.	nostri/nostrum
dat.	nobis
abl.	nobis

130 tu/vos 'you'

Singular

nom.	tu
acc.	te
gen.	tui
dat.	tibi
abl.	te

Plural

nom.	vos
acc.	vos
gen.	vestri/vestrum
dat.	vobis
abl.	vobis

131 is (m) ea (f) id (n) 'he, she, it'

Singular

nom.	is, ea, id
acc.	eum, eam, id
gen.	eius (all)
dat.	ei (all)
abl.	eo, ea, eo

Plural

nom.	ei, eae, ea
acc.	eos, eas, ea
gen.	eorum earum, eorum
dat.	eis (all)
abl.	eis (all)

ADJECTIVES

THE TWO TYPES

132 2ND/1ST DECLENSION ADJECTIVES
(bon-us bon-a bon-um)

167

Masculine singular (like serv-us, 125)
nom. bon-us
voc. bon-e
acc. bon-um
gen. bon-i
dat. bon-o
abl. bon-o

Masculine plural
nom. bon-i
voc. bon-i
acc. bon-os
gen. bon-orum
dat. bon-is
abl. bon-is

Feminine singular (like serv-a, 124)
nom. bon-a
voc. bon-a
acc. bon-am
gen. bon-ae
dat. bon-ae
abl. bon-a

Feminine plural
nom. bon-ae
voc. bon-ae
acc. bon-as
gen. bon-arum
dat. bon-is
abl. bon-is

Neuter singular (like bell-um, 126)
nom. bon-um
voc. bon-um
acc. bon-um
gen. bon-i
dat. bon-o
abl. bon-o

Neuter plural
nom. bon-a
voc. bon-a
acc. bon-a
gen. bon-orum
dat. bon-is
abl. bon-is

133 3RD DECLENSION ADJECTIVES
(omnis)

Masculine and feminine singular (endings like dux, 127, but n.b. abl. s and gen. pl)

nom.	omn-is
voc.	omn-is
acc.	omn-em
gen.	omn-is
dat.	omn-i
abl.	omn-i

Masculine and feminine plural

nom.	omn-es
voc.	omn-es
acc.	omn-es
gen.	omn-ium
dat.	omn-ibus
abl.	omn-ibus

Neuter singular

nom.	omn-e
voc.	omn-e
acc.	omn-e
gen.	omn-is
dat.	omn-i
abl.	omn-i

Neuter plural

nom.	omn-ia
voc.	omn-ia
acc.	omn-ia
gen.	omn-ium
dat.	omn-ibus
abl.	omn-ibus

RECORDED VOCABULARY
Latin-English

<u>Key</u>

1v, 2v etc. = first, second (etc.) conjugation verb; **v irr** = irregular verb.
n. 1f = noun, first declension, feminine; **n. 2m** = noun, second declension, masculine; **n. 2n** = noun, second declension neuter; **n. 3m/f/n.** = noun, third declension, masculine/feminine/neuter.
adj. 2/1 = adjective, first and second declension type; **adj. 3** = adjective, third declension type.
Long vowels are marked with a bar.

a(b) + abl., by (a person)
absēns absent- adj. 3 absent
accipi-ō 5v accip-ere accēp-ī accept-um take, receive
ad + acc., towards, near, in
am-ō 1v amā-re amāv-ī amāt-um love, like
amor amor- n. 3m love
angel-us n. 2m angel
Angl-us n. 2m Englishman, Angle
anim-a n. 1f life, soul
apprehend-ō 3v apprehend-ere apprehend-ī apprehēns-um seize
aqu-a n. 1f water
audi-ō 4v audī-re audīv-ī audīt-um hear, listen
autem however, but
avē (s) avēte (pl) welcome! hail!
bell-um n. 2n war
bon-us a um adj. 2/1 good
cad-ō 3v cad-ere cecid-ī fall, die
cael-um n. 2n sky, heaven
capi-ō 5v cap-ere cēp-ī capt-um capture
caput capit- n. 3n head
Christ-us n. 2m Christ
cib-us n. 2m food
clām-ō 1v clāmāre clāmāvī shout
col-ō 3v col-ere colu-ī cult-um inhabit
coqu-ō 3v coqu-ere cook
contrā + acc. against
cor cord- n. 3n heart

Corinn-a n. 1f Corinna
corōn-a n. 1f crown
corpus corpor- n. 3n body
cre-ō 1v creā-re creāv-i creāt-um create
crucifīg-ō 3v crucifīg-ere crucifix-ī
crux cruc- n. 3f cross
cum + abl., (in company) with; + subjunctive, since, when
cūr why?
custōdi-ō 4v custōdī-re custōdīv-ī custōdīt-um guard
Cynthi-a n. 1f Cynthia
dēbet he ought
Dēli-a n. 1f Delia
de-us n. 2m god
dīc (s) dīcite (pl) say!, speak!
dīc-ō 3v dīc-ere dīx-ī dict-um say, speak
dīlig-ō 3v dīlig-ere dīlēx-ī dīlēct-um love
dīmitt-ō 3v dīmitt-ere dīmīs-ī let go, release
discipul-us n. 2m disciple
d-ō 1v dā-re ded-ī dat-um give
duc (s) ducite (pl) lead!
duc-ō 3v duc-ere dux-ī duct-um lead
dum while
dux duc- n. 3m general, leader, Duke
eā n. abl. s (with) (by) her
eam n. acc. s her
eās n. acc. pl them (f)

eārum n. gen pl of them, their (f)
ecce see! behold!
ecclēsi-a n. 1f church
ego I
ei n. dat. s to him, to her, to it
eis n. dat. and abl. pl, to them, (by)
(with) them
eius n. gen. s of him, of her, of it; his,
her(s), its
eō v ire ĭ(v)-ī it-um go
eō n. abl s (by) (with) him
eōrum n. gen pl of them, their (m)
eōs n. acc. l them (m)
eum n. acc. s him
equit-ō 1v equitā-re equitāv-ī equitāt-
um ride
era- imperfect stem of sum
ergō therefore
es you are
est he/she/it is
estis you (pl) are
et and
eunt they go
e(x) + abl., out of
exeō v irr exīre exĭ(v)ī exit-um depart from, leave
exercit-us n. 4m army
fac (s) facite (pl) make! do!
faci-ō 5v fac-ere fēc-ī fact-um make,
do
festīn-ō 1v festīnā-re festīnāv-ī festī-
nāt-um hurry
fle-ō 2v flē-re cry
fīli-us n. 2m son
formōs-us a um adj. 2/1 beautiful
fort-is adj. 3 brave
fortūn-a n. 1f fortune, luck
frater fratr- n. 3m brother
fu- perfect stem of sum
fugā vert-ō 3v vertere vert-ī vers-um
turn in flight
habe-ō 2v habē-re habu-ī habit-um
have
Harold-us n. 2m Harold
hĭc here
homō homin- n. 3m man, fellow
iam now, already
ib- imperfect stem of eō
impon-ō 3v impōn-ere imposu-ī impo-
sit-um place X (acc.) on Y (dat.)
in + acc., into
in + abl., in

incend-ō 3v incend-ere burn
inimĭc-us n. 2m (personal) enemy
interfici-ō 5v interfic-ere interfēc-ī interfect-um kill
interrog-ō 1v interrogā-re interrogāv-ī
interrogāt-um question
iube-ō 2v iubē-re iuss-ī iuss-um
īs you go
it he/she/it goes
īmus we go
ĭtis you (pl) go
ĭ(v)- perfect stem of eō
lex leg- n. 3f law
loc-us n. 2m place
long-us a um adj. 2/1 long, tall
lūn-a n. 1f moon
magn-us a um adj. 2/1 great, big
malle to prefer
malō v irr malle malu-ī prefer
malu- perfect stem of malō
malūmus we prefer
malunt they prefer
mal-us a um adj. 2/1 bad, wicked, evil
mare mar- n. 3n sea
māter matr- n. 3f mother
māvis you prefer
māvult he/she/it prefers
māvultis you (pl) prefer
mē n. acc. s, abl s. me
mēcum with me
mei n. gen. s of me
mēns ment- n. 3f mind
me-us a um adj. 2/1 my, mine
mihi n. dat. s to me
mīles mīlit- n. 3m soldier
ministr-ō 1v ministrā-re ministrāv-ī
ministrāt-um serve
miser miser-a miser-um adj. 2/1 unhappy
mitt-ō 3v mitt-ere mīs-ī miss-um send
modo now
mone-ō 2v monē-re monu-ī monit-um
advise, warn
monument-um n. 2n tomb
mulier mulier- n. 3f woman, wife
mult-us a um adj. 2/1 much, (pl)
many
mund-us n. 2m world
nāv-is nav- n. 3f ship
nesci-ō 4v nesci-re nescīv-ī nescĭt-um
know not, do not know
niger nigr-a um adj. 2/1 black

nisi unless
nōbil-is adj. 3 noble
nōbīscum with us
nōlī (s), nōlīte (pl) don't! (+ infinitive)
nōl-ō v irr nōlle nōlu-ī refuse, do not wish/want
nōlu-ī perfect stem of nōlō
nōlūmus we refuse
nōlunt they refuse
Normann-us n. 2m Norman
nōbīs n. dat. and abl. pl to us, (by) (with) us
nōs n. nom. and acc. pl we, us
noster nostr-a -um adj. 2/1 our(s)
nostrī, nostrum n. gen. pl of us, our(s)
not-ō 1v notā-re notāv-i notāt-um note, mark
nunc now
nūnti-ō 1v nūntiā-re nūntiāv-i nūntiāt-um (v) tell, announce
ōd-ī (perfect in form, present in meaning) I hate
ōlim once upon a time
omn-is adj. 3 every, (pl) all
palāti-um n. 2n palace
parv-us a um adj. 2/1 small, (pl) few
pater patr- n. 3m father
per + acc. through
pōn-ō 3v pōn-ere posu-ī place
plōr-ō 1v plōrā-re weep
pontifex pontific- n. 3m leader, high priest
port-ō 1v portā-re portāv-ī portāt-um carry
possum posse potu-ī am able, can
post + acc. after
potestās potestāt- n. 3f power
potu- perfect stem of possum
praepar-ō 1v praeparā-re prepare
prandi-um n. 2n dinner
prīncipi-um n. 2n beginning, principle
proeli-um n. 2n battle
proptereā therefore
puell-a n. 1f girl
pugn-ō 1v pugnā-re pugnāv-ī pugnāt-um fight
pulcher pulchr-a um adj. 2/1 beautiful
quae grātia what thanks?
quaer-ō 3v quaer-ere seek
quia because, that

quid what?
quī who
quis who?
reg-ō 3v reg-ere rex-ī rect-um rule
resideō 2v residē-re sit down
respōns-um n. 2n reply
rēx rēg- n. 3m king
salvē (s) salvēte (pl) welcome! hail!
sānct-us n. 2m saint (also adj. 2/1 holy)
sapienti-a n. 1f wisdom
sci-ō 4v scī-re scīv-ī scīt-um know
scrīb-ō 3v scrīb-ere scrīps-ī scrīpt-um write
sē him(self), her(self), them(selves) (referring to the subject of the sentence)
sed but
sede-ō 2v sedē-re sit
semper always
senti-ō 4v sentī-re sēns-ī sēns-um
sermo sermōn- n. 3m conversation, words
serv-a n. 1f (female) slave
serv-us n. 2m (male) slave
sī if
soror soror- n. 3f sister
stell-a n. 1f star
sum v irr esse fu-ī I am
sumus we are
sunt they are
tang-ō 3v tang-ere touch
tē n. acc. s, abl. s you (s)
tēcum with you (s)
tenebr-a n. 1f shadow
tene-ō 2v tenē-re tenu-ī tent-um hold, take
terr-a n. 1f earth, land
tibi n. dat. s to you
tōt-us a um adj. 2/1 complete(ly), total(ly)
trād-ō 3v trād-ere trādid-ī hand over, give up
trah-ō 3v trah-ere trax-ī tract-um drag
transeō v irr transīre cross
trīst-is adj. 3 sad
tū n. nom. s you (s)
tuī n. gen s of you, your(s)
tu-us a um adj. 2/1 your(s) (when you = one person)
tunc then

172

ubi where, when

ut in order that; (after verbs of commanding, persuading, etc.) that ... should

valē (s) valēte (pl) farewell! good bye!

veni-ō 4v venī-re vēn-ī vent-um

vester vestr-a um adj. 2/1 your(s) (when you = more than one person)

vestrī, vestrum n. gen pl of you, your(s)

vide-ō 2v vidē-re vĭd-ī vīs-um see

vinc-ō 3v vinc-ere vīc-ī vict-um conquer

vīn-um n. 2n wine

virgō virgin- 3f young girl

vīs you (s) wish

vīt-a n. 1f life

vīv-ō 3v vīv-ere live

vōbīs n. dat. and abl. pl to you, (by) (with) you

vōbīscum with you (pl)

volūmus we wish

vol-ō v irr velle volu-ī wish, want

volunt they wish

volv-ō 3v volv-ere roll, turn

vōs n. nom. and acc. pl you

vult he/she/it wishes

vultis you (pl) wish

Willelm-us (many different spellings) n. 2m William

RECORDED VOCABULARY
English-Latin

Note
Verbs: to construct **present** and **imperfect indicative**, and **present infinitive** and **imperative** forms, you need to know the **present** stem and conjugation. You need to know the **3rd p.p.** to construct **perfect** and **pluperfect active** forms, and the **4th p.p.** to construct **perfect** and **pluperfect passive** forms. **sum, possum, eo, volo, nolo, malo** are irr. throughout and need to be looked up separately.

Nouns: nouns follow their declension type. Declension type determines **stem** and **ending**. 1st declension nouns follow 1st declension rules, etc. Remember that the stem of 3rd declension nouns cannot be predicted and must be known.

Verb key
1 = first conjugation, with p.p.s on the pattern am-o ama-re amav-i amat-um.
2 = second conjugation, with p.p.s on the pattern mone-o mone-re monu-i monit-um.
3, 5 = third and fifth conjugation, all with irregular 3rd and 4th p.p.s: look these up in Latin-English vocabulary.
4 = fourth conjugation, with p.p.s on the pattern audi-o audi-re audiv-i audit-um.
The p.p.s of **1, 2** and **4** conj. verbs are regular, unless irr. is added. Look these up in the Latin-English section.

advise moneo 2
always semper
announce nuntio 1
ask interrogo 1
battle proeli-um 2n
be sum irr.
be able possum irr.
believe credo 3
but sed
can possum irr.
capture capio 5
carry porto 1

come venio 4 irr.
conquer vinco 3
Corinna Corinn-a 1f
could: use (im)perfect of possum
create creo 1
Cynthia Cynthi-a 1f
Delia Deli-a 1f
delight delecto 1
dinner prandi-um 2n
do facio 5
don't! noli (s), nolite (pl) (+ infinitive)
drag traho 3
farewell vale (s), valete (pl)
father pater patr- 3m
feel sentio 4 irr.
fellow homo homin- 3m
fight pugno 1
general dux duc- 3m
give do 1 irr.
go eo irr.
guard custodio 4
have habeo 2
have been: use perfect of sum
hear audio 4
her eam (acc.)
here hic
him eum (acc.)
hold teneo 2
hurry festino 1

I ego
into in + acc.
king rex reg- 3m
know scio 4
lead duco 3
leader dux duc- 3m
listen audio 4
love amo 1
make facio 5
mother mater matr- 3f
no(t) non
not know nescio 4
not want, wish nolo irr.
now nunc
order iubeo 2 irr
palace palati-um 2n
prefer malo irr.
question interrogo 1
refuse nolo irr.
reply respondeo 2 irr.
ride equito 1
rule rego 3
say dico 3
see video 2 irr.
seize apprehendo 3
send mitto 3
serve servo 1
ship navis nav- 3f

slave-girl serv-a 1f
soldier miles milit- 3m
speak dico 3
stand sto 1 irr.
star stell-a 1f
take teneo 2
tell dico 3
terrify terreo 2
to: if motion, use ad + acc; if not, use
    dative case.
towards ad + acc.
want volo irr.
warn moneo 2
was: use perfect or imperfect of sum
was able: use (im)perfect of possum
was/were -ing: use imperfect tense of
    verb of -ing.
we nos
welcome salve (s), salvete (pl)
went: use perfect of eo
what? quid?
who? quis?
why? cur?
wish volo irr.
woman mulier mulier- 3f
you (s) tu, (pl) vos
young girl virgo virgin- 3f

GRAMMATICAL INDEX

References are to sections of chapters (1b, 7c etc). The *Grammatical Summary* contains all verb, noun and adjective forms.